Felting
by Hand

Anne Einset Vickrey

Craft Works Publishing
Palo Alto, California

*In memory of my grandmother Tomine N. Rønneberg,
who introduced me to the fun of hand crafts.*

Designer   *Beverly Kennon-Kelley*
Editors   *Anne Lewis*
                Christine Losq
                James F. Vickrey
Illustrator   *Vicky Nuttall*
Compositor *Meredith Hoffman*
Technique photos, photo of author and cover photography   *Tony Coluzzi*
Photo on page 60   *John F. Madden*
Outdoor photography and photos of finished articles   *Anne E. Vickrey*

Library of Congress Cataloging-in-Publication Data

Vickrey, Anne Einset, 1951-
    Felting by Hand

    Bibliography: p.
    1. Felting.   2. Felt work.   I. Title.
TT849.5.V53 1987   746'.0463   87-19912

ISBN 0-9619053-5-2

Ordering information on last page.

10 9 8 7 6 5 4

Printed in the United States of America

Acknowledgements

I first want to thank my teacher, Annelise Stockflet Jørgensen, for teaching me how to felt and for being an inspiration. She is a rare person of many talents and much knowledge. I wish we lived closer to each other. I want also to thank the students to whom I have had the privilege of teaching felting. It is from them that I have received the most reward and understanding of what is important in teaching the technique. Many people have helped me further the craft: I want to thank Ede Riesenhuber for her help with finding domestic sources of wool for felting; Lyn Dearborn for organizing workshops and providing resources; and Karen Livingstone for helping with the dyeing portion of the book by providing her dye studio for experimentation and for dyeing fleece and felt. I want to thank Karen most of all for her interest and moral support in my business enterprise.

In preparing this book, many people have been of the utmost help. I want to thank Vi Elliott for typing the major portion of the manuscript. I would also like to thank my brother, Erik Einset, for the photography in the first short version.

Finally I want to thank my family for their help, without which I could have never completed this book. First to my husband, for his patience and help with computers and editing. Then to my mother, who has always been very encouraging throughout the process of getting the book together. Finally to my children, Rebecca and John, who have been patient when I have had to spend weekends working on the book. They have also happily served as models for the clothes I have made for them—even when the California climate was not suited to woolen clothing.

Contents

Introduction

Felting is a simple technique by which you can make wonderfully warm wool items to wear. The main advantage felting has over other textile techniques is producing a finished article in much less time. If you have ever watched someone make felt, you have seen how quickly different items can be made.

No one knows for certain how man first discovered the felting properties of wool, but several ideas suggest how early man may have become interested in making felt. Matted wool may have been noticed on sheep. Wool shed from wild sheep may have been found formed into a matted mass of fibers as a result of the elements. Perhaps man stuffed his footwear, presumably animal hide, with wool to keep his feet warm. After walking on the wool for a while, he found that it became stiff and formed a kind of fabric.

The oldest archaeological finds containing evidence of the use of felt are in Turkey. Wall paintings that date from 6500 to 6300 B.C. have been found which have the motif of felt appliqué. The earliest felt found in Scandinavia dates back to the Iron Age. Felt sheets believed to be from about 500 A.D.were found covering a body in a tomb in Hordaland, Norway. The Icelandic sagas of early medieval times mention the use of felt saddles and garments. The Romans and Greeks knew of felt. Roman soldiers were equipped with felt breastplates, tunics, boots, and socks.

Today, felt is an important part of life in many parts of the Middle East. It is used for items ranging from clothing to the walls of tents. The extensive use of felt stems in part from the fact that you need very few materials and equipment to make felt. Most of the projects described here, for example, require only wool, soap, water, and perhaps a washboard.

This book is written for the beginner who wants to make handmade felt. It is also meant to inspire the reader as he or she becomes more experienced at felting. The beginning chapters of the book give more detailed information about the procedure for making the items, and later chapters present detailed instructions for making slippers, boots, mittens, and hats. The beginner should read through the chapters on wool, equipment, carding, and patterns before starting the step-by-step procedures for making any of the felt items for wear.

As is often stressed in the book, the key to success with handmade felt items for wear is using the right kind of wool. Any wool will felt into a little piece after you work on it long enough, but in order to shape a slipper, for example, you need wool that felts quickly into material which is firm enough for wear. Several sheep breeds produce wool with this quality. As explained in Chapter 1, the sheep breeds you find in the United States are most likely crosses of two or more breeds. Because the wool quality varies from sheep to sheep, it is impossible to say that one or another breed is better for felting. The only way to determine the felting quality of a fleece is to make a sample. However, after testing fleece from a variety of breeds of sheep available in the United States, the author recommends several breeds whose wool is more likely to be good for felting. If you do not have access to these breeds, the Appendix lists sources of wool for felting.

When making felt, the goal is to get the fabric as even as possible and to keep the shape of the article as close to the pattern as possible. Proper carding, even batts, and correct felting technique are all important for achieving this goal. Chapter 2 explains how to card wool for felting and describes the procedure for mixing wools from two different breeds of sheep. Table 1-1 in Chapter 1 gives suggestions for types of wool to use when blending, and Table 1-2 suggests various articles you can make from different types of wool.

Compared to other fiber crafts, very little equipment is needed for felting, but some aids may be helpful. Chapter 3 presents the equipment list and explains the purpose of each item as it relates to making felt.

After obtaining wool you wish to use for felting, you should make a sample before starting a larger project. You will get an idea of how well your wool will felt and, very importantly, how fast it will felt. Follow the suggestions in Chapter 4 for making samples, and refer to Chapter 1 to determine

what type of wool you have. If you have no experience at felting by hand, you should first make a small piece of felt to get a feel for the technique before starting on a project.

In Chapter 5, the basics of making patterns are presented. After reading this chapter you will be able to make a pattern for slippers, boots, mittens, or a hat. As a beginner, you may want to start with one of the patterns in the book (see Appendix D), but making your own patterns is not difficult.

Chapters 6 and 7 introduce the felting and fulling processes. The descriptions and illustrations help explain the changes you will feel in the wool as it becomes felt. As with any craft or skill, the more you practice this technique, the better your final result will be.

As you become inspired to make more things out of felt after you try the items in this book, Chapter 9 gives suggestions for other projects, and Chapter 10 describes several children's projects. However, you will undoubtedly think of your own uses of felt along the way. Chapters 11 and 12 explain how to wash your felt wearables and provide ideas for decorating the items you make as you create truly personalized pieces of clothing.

To get started at felting you will find sources of carded wool in Appendix A. If you have your own sheep or have fleece (unwashed wool directly from the sheep) available to you, there is a source list in Appendix C for where you can send the wool to be carded. Sources for wool are suggested in Appendix B.

1
Choosing the Best Wool
for Felting

For the beginning felter, the most common cause of discouragement is working with the wrong kind of wool. You need to use wool that felts quickly and easily to make felt articles like slippers, hats, mittens, and boots. Do not expect good results from poor quality wool that you wouldn't use for anything else. Avoid dead-pulled wool and wool that is too dirty. When using dog hair, angora, or hair from any other animal, be sure to mix it with at least half again as much sheep's wool. In Appendix A you can find several sources for felting wool. However, part of the fun and challenge of felting is experimenting with wool readily available to you.

The sheep breeds in the United States differ from the European breeds whose wool is used for felting in Scandinavia. In addition, the wool from the Romney breed, which is commonly used for felting in New Zealand, will not always be suitable when found locally. Because it is not possible to predict felting quality of local breeds, the author tested a variety of fleeces to identify wools available in California that are suitable for felting. Lincoln crossbreeds and some other breeds that are considered to be "coarse" by the American Wool Grading System have shown to be the best for felting. Wool that is good for felting has a sheen or luster. Blending this wool with a finer wool provides a mixed fleece with the characteristics you need for felting.

Most sheep found in this country are crossbreeds and may be related to breeds which produce wool that is good for felting. The rate at which the wool felts when following the technique in this book may be fast, medium, or slow, or a combination of these. How you can best use the wool you have available depends on how fast the wool felts. For example, in order to make a large item like a hat, you need wool that felts quickly (fast-felting). Wool requiring a longer period of time to felt (medium-felting) will work, but because the fibers do not felt as quickly, the hat is more likely to stretch while you are working on it. This will require that you shrink the hat much longer on the washboard. When making a smaller item like a slipper, medium-felting wool is preferable to fast-felting wool so that your project does not shrink too quickly, resulting in a slipper that is too small.

In order to better explain the differences in wools used for felting, this book uses categories to describe the different felting rates: fast-felting, medium-felting, or slow-felting. Most wools fall into the last category and thus are not good by themselves for felting. However, these slow-felting wools can be used for felting when mixed with a wool from the first or second group. Try the wool you have available by making a sample (see Chapter 4). This will help you decide which category it belongs in and what items you can make with it (see Table 1-2). In many cases, mixing wools from different categories improves the felting qualities of both.

Three Categories of Wool for Felting

Fast-Felting Wool

Wool that felts quickly when you work with it falls into the fast-felting category. When using this wool, your finished product may not need to be toughened, or fulled (see Chapter 7), on the washboard. However, when you make larger items like boots or hats, these need to be toughened so that they hold their shape. The finished product is a firmer felt that can be made quite thin. To make a puffier, thicker material, mix fast-felting wool with wool that does not felt by itself (slow-felting wool). In addition, do not rub it as much, if at all, on the washboard. The larger you make a piece, the more fast-felting wool you want. This is for two reasons:

- First, fast-felting wool shrinks quickly and to a thinner and denser felt than slower felting wool. Therefore, you need to start with a larger pattern and more wool.

- Second, since a larger project takes more time to felt than a smaller project, using fast-felting wool will decrease the time required to finish the project.

Medium-Felting Wool

This wool can be used for any type of project. When blending different fleeces, the goal is to obtain a wool with felting qualities in this range. It will take a little longer for this wool to felt, but after being rubbed on a washboard it will give the same results as fast-felting wool. To make a thicker, puffier material using the same weight of wool, do not rub on the washboard very long, if at all. However, if the slippers or boots have stretched out of shape during the felting process, they can be shrunk to the desired size by continuing to rub them on the washboard during the fulling process.

Slow-Felting Wool

The main characteristic of this type of wool is that it will felt into a small, flat sample, but it will not hold together when making a slipper or other item. You will not be able to complete any of the projects with this wool alone. Although it may seem to hold together in spots, it will fall apart when rubbed on the washboard. Slow-felting wool needs to be mixed with fast- or medium-felting wool before you can use it. Starting your first project with only slow-felting wool is very discouraging—you can work and work on it and very little will happen. This wool has its purposes in felting, however, as stated before; it is perfect for mixing with fast- or medium-felting wool to make a thicker, puffier felt material, and it slows down the felting rate of fast-felting wool to give you more control over the shrinkage of your project.

Table 1-1 summarizes the author's experience with testing the felting rates of various sheep breeds available in California. Table 1-2 relates felting rates of the different wools with specific projects.

TABLE 1-1.
FELTING RATES OF VARIOUS DOMESTIC SHEEP BREEDS

Sheep Breeds	Felting Time	Needs Fulling*	Needs Blending	Comments
Dorset	Slow	Will not felt.	Yes, to improve felting.	This wool needs to be mixed, as it will not felt by itself. Mix it with Lincoln or Lincoln crosses (medium or fast).
Romney Crossbreeds	Slow to Medium	The finer crossbreeds will not felt. Coarser crossbreeds need fulling.	Yes, to improve felting.	This wool needs to be mixed when using a finer fleece.
Corriedale	Medium Slow	Yes	Yes, to improve felting with slow-felting wool.	Mixing this wool with one-quarter Lincoln greatly improves the results.
Border Leicester	Medium	Yes	No	This wool will shed and is slippery to work with. It is best to mix it with a finer wool.
Lincoln	Fast to Medium	Yes	Yes, to improve felting.	This wool will shed and is slippery to work with. It is best to mix it with a finer wool.
Lincoln Crossbreeds	Medium Fast	Sometimes	No	A fleece with more Lincoln characteristics (i.e., luster) felts best.
Lincoln/Corriedale/Dorset Cross	Fast	No
Yes, for hats.	Yes, to slow felting.	This particular fleece felts very fast. It is good for blending with other wools to speed up their felting rates.
Mixed wools of 50% Adult Mohair Goat 50% Dorset	Medium	Will not full well on the washboard.	Use less than one-half Mohair because of slipperiness.	An equal mix of Mohair and Dorset (slow) wools formed a felt material fairly quickly (medium); however, it is hard to keep the shape because of the slipperiness of the Mohair. It makes a very soft material but the Mohair sheds.

*Fulling—the shrinking and shaping of the felt on a washboard to harden it—is described in chapter 7.

TABLE 1-2.
SUGGESTED WOOL TYPES FOR MAKING DIFFERENT ARTICLES

Fast	Medium-Fast	Medium	Medium-Slow	Slow
Hats	Hats	Larger-sized Slippers	Smaller Items: Slippers Mittens	Not suitable by itself.
	Boots			
		Boots		
Larger Items: Vests Wall Hangings		Larger-sized Mittens		

2
Preparing Your Wool

One of the first steps in making felt is to lay out the wool you will be using. This is done by layering your carded wool into uniform quantities or batts. Careful carding of the wool for your batts and laying down the wool evenly into batts are important steps for obtaining an even material. Ideally, the carded wool for your batts should be puffy and in fairly thin layers.

Carding Wool for Felting

Hand-Carded Wool

When carding by hand, do not put more than a half ounce of lightly washed wool on your carders at one time.

Card the wool until the fibers are all going in one direction. Transfer the wool from one carder to the other while carding.

Remove the wool from the carders in a flat sheet, and lay it on a flat surface.

Continue to pile up your carded wool until you have the amount you need for your project.

Drum-Carded Wool or Roving

Wool prepared in this way can also be used for felting. Pick the wool fibers apart so the wool is fed into the drum carder uniformly.

Avoid uneven areas by putting the wool through the carder more than once.

Remember that you want very light and airy batts, so the wool should be pulled apart to make at least 4 to 5 layers for each batt.

Commercially-Carded Wool Batts

Comforter or quilt batts may also be used for felting as long as the wool has been blended for this purpose (see the source list in Appendix A). The fibers in the batt have been carded so they are all lying in the same direction. Carefully pull the layers apart for making the batts to be used for felting.

Blending Wools

If you are starting with hand- or drum-carded fleece, you will most likely need to blend your wool for felting. To obtain the medium-felting wool that many of the projects need, you can blend fast-felting wool with slow-felting wool. You can also test how well your wool works for felting when it is blended. In any case, the fibers need to be well mixed.

Hand-Carded Wool

When hand carding, the wool is blended by putting together some of each wool type on your carder and slightly carding it together. Transfer the wool from one carder to the other two or three times while combing it out. Remove the wool and mix again by pulling it apart with your hands. Then the wool can be carded again to form the sheets you will use in your batts.

Drum-Carded Wool

Before drum carding, pick the lightly washed wool apart with your fingers so it is very light and airy. When you are ready to card it, put an equal amount of each wool type through the drum carder at the same time. Pull the carded wool apart lengthwise and put it through the drum carder two more times.

Making Batts

Depending on how your wool was carded, the method for making batts varies. When you prepare the carded wool for laying down on the batts, never use scissors to cut the wool—always pull it apart.

Start with thin layers for your batts.

Hand-Carded Wool

When using hand-carded wool, first place your cotton pattern on a flat surface and, according to the step-by-step directions in Chapter 8, lay the carded wool on top of the pattern. The sheets that you remove flat from the carders should all be about equal weight. Lay them down so each layer of the batt has wool lying in a "shingle" or overlapping pattern. Start at one edge, allowing 1½ inches of wool to extend out from the pattern. Overlap the next row about a third. Lay the fibers in the second layer perpendicular to those in the first layer (see figures below). Check for thin areas in the batts, and while you pile the layers of wool add more wool to areas you think may be thin. To prevent having thin areas that could result in holes or thin spots in the finished material, be sure to card the wool evenly. Hold the batt up to a light to check for uniformity. Make all the batts at once for a project to ensure uniformity in your projects (for example, prepare four batts for a pair of slippers).

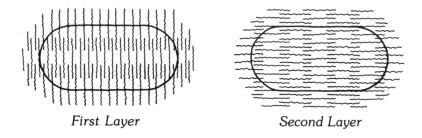

First Layer   *Second Layer*

Drum-Carded Wool

Depending on how wide the drum carder is, you may be able to make each layer of the batt in one piece. Light and airy batts are important for an even material, so the drum-carded wool should be pulled apart to make thin layers. As with batts made with other methods of carding, there should be four to five layers of wool in each batt. If one piece does not cover the pattern, overlap where you lay down more than one piece.

Commercially-Carded Batts

If you use commercially carded batts, it is likely that each layer will be in one piece, much like drum-carded wool. If you do not have a piece big enough for one layer, overlap where you lay more wool down. Never cut the wool with scissors—always tear it apart, first in the direction of the fibers, then across the fibers, to get the size of batt you need.

3
Equipment

Felt material can be made using very little equipment. This is probably one of the reasons why it became the first manmade fabric. All that is needed to make felt for clothing, tents, or other items is wool, solid or liquid soap, and hot water. Ideally, these three things are all that are needed for starting this hobby. However, additional equipment that will help you when you make felt items for wear are suggested below.

Wooden Cutting Board

This board should be fairly smooth and large enough so that there is at least two to three inches of room all around your pattern. Put a folded towel or washcloth under one end to raise it slightly so that the water will drain off when you are working on your project.

Pan (or insulated bottle) for hot, soapy water

The water should be hot when you put it on your project, so an insulated bottle (such as a Thermos bottle) is handy to use. Otherwise, you may have to make up a new bowl of hot, soapy water halfway through the felting process.

Scale

You can use the scale for weighing out the total wool for a project and to make sure each batt is equal in weight. This helps ensure that your items will

be even and that one slipper or boot will be the same thickness as the second one. A small dietetic scale is sufficient. Use the top of a shoe box to hold the wool while it is being weighed.

Cotton Fabric

You need the cotton fabric to make your pattern. Using fabric that is a different color than your wool helps you find the pattern when you come to the step where you cut into the wool.

Scissors

These are needed for cutting into your felted wool to reach the pattern. A pair of sharp-pointed scissors makes it easy to cut straight into the wool.

Washboard or Felting Board

Rubbing your slipper, hat, or other project on a washboard or felting board (similar to a washboard) quickly shrinks it in areas where needed. The wool will shrink in the direction that you rub—this means you have control over where and how much shrinkage you get. Your project should first be felted by hand before rubbing it on the washboard. If it is not felted enough, or if your wool is not suitable for felting, your project will pull apart when you rub it on the washboard.

Soap

The felting of wool is accomplished by the presence of heat, a slightly alkaline solution, and continuous manipulation of the fibers. Soap provides the alkalinity that is chemically necessary for the felting process. It also allows your hands to slide over the wool and make the manipulative process easier. Laundry soap is the most economical, and be sure to use soap instead of detergent. The soap you use should feel greasy when it is dissolved in the hot water. If your water is very hard, it will take more soap to achieve that greasy feeling. When this is the case, add one-quarter teaspoon of baking soda to one quart of hot water along with your soap powder or flakes.

To make your soap solution, measure out:

- ¼ cup soap powder or flakes

- 2 quarts hot water (as hot as your hands can stand)

Combine these two ingredients. It normally takes about three to four quarts of hot, soapy water to prepare felt for a pair of slippers or boots. Liquid soap will also work, but it is more expensive.

These slipper samples show the felting rates of various fleeces—starting with slow-felting at the bottom and moving to fast-felting at the top.

4
Making Felt Samples

Before you spend a lot of time carding and making batts, you must determine how well the wool you plan to use will felt. The best way to determine this is to make a sample. A felt sample may be made in a flat piece or shaped into a small slipper. When making the sample, keep in mind the characteristics of fast-, medium-, and slow-felting wool (explained in Chapter 2).

Flat Sample

With at least two-thirds of an ounce of carded wool, make a small batt using five to six layers of wool. Pour one-eighth cup of hot, soapy water into the middle of the batt and wet down most of the wool—keep two inches of the batt dry all around the edge. Fold the dry wool over the wet wool and wet it down. Felt the sample following the procedure in Chapter 6. Within 10 to 15 minutes, the sample should turn to felt.

Slipper Sample

If you have a large quantity of wool—a whole fleece, for example—the best way to determine its felting quality is to make a small slipper. This will give you a better idea as to how well the wool can be shaped. Start with the sample pattern provided in Appendix D or a small pattern about five to six inches long and three inches wide. Round the pattern at the ends. Follow the step-by-step instructions for making a slipper in Chapter 8.

What to Look for When Making a Sample

Slow-Felting Wool

If the wool never really gets "hard" and just holds together slightly, it is slow-felting wool which is not suitable by itself for felting.

Medium-Felting Wool

Medium-felting wool begins to hold together after working on it for about ten minutes. It shrinks quickly on the washboard with hot, soapy water and becomes a firm fabric.

Fast-Felting Wool

Fast-felting wool becomes firm or hardens so quickly that you can stand on a batt and pull the wool up around your foot to felt it into a slipper. It is very rewarding to work with because you get such quick results.

After you have made a sample and have decided which type of wool you have, check Table 1-2 to decide which projects suit it best.

5
Making Your Own Patterns

The patterns for the items in this book are guides to shape and size. However, because some wools will shrink more than others, the size of the pattern not only depends on your foot, hand, or head size, but also on your wool. If you are a beginner and are using fast-felting wool, you may find that your finished product is smaller than desired. Compensate by making a pattern large enough to allow for shrinkage. You may also need to start with more fast-felting wool because of the larger pattern size and its tendency to make a tighter and stronger fabric. With medium-felting wool, you should start with a pattern that is close to the size with which you wish to end. On the other hand, if you are working with wool that is especially slow to felt, your slipper may stretch out while you work on it, so starting with a smaller pattern will help. Table 5-1 summarizes the general rules for pattern sizes and the amount of wool to use when making a felt wearable from any of the three types of wool.

TABLE 5-1.
ADJUSTING YOUR PATTERN TO THE WOOL TYPE

Wool Type	Pattern Size	Amount of Wool to Use
Fast-felting wool	Larger pattern	Use more wool
Medium-felting wool	Pattern near foot size	Follow instructions
Slow-felting wool	Smaller pattern	Follow instructions

Making a Pattern for Slippers

Step 1. When making a pattern for slippers, first trace one of the feet of the person you want the slipper to fit. Have that person stand on a hard surface (not a rug), then trace the foot as you hold your pen or pencil straight up and down. Be sure to use a piece of paper that extends at least 2 inches all around the foot.

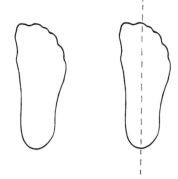

Step 2. Look at the tracing and determine the midline of the foot.

Step 3. Draw a line lengthwise down the middle of the foot tracing.

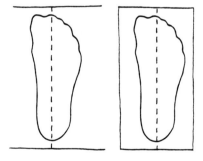

Step 4. Draw a line 1 inch from the tip of the big toe, perpendicular to the midline of the foot. Do the same thing 1 inch from the heel.

Step 5. Repeat with the sides of the foot so that you have drawn a rectangle with the foot tracing centered in the middle.

Step 6. Cut out the rectangle and fold the paper in half lengthwise, keeping the tracing on the outside. Fold the paper in half again as shown. You should have one-quarter of the foot tracing showing.

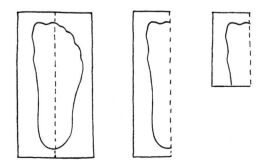

Step 7. With your scissors, cut off the four corners at the same time with one rounded cut. When you open up the paper, check that it is symmetrical and that the ends are rounded. You should have an average of three-quarters of an inch of paper all around the tracing. At the widest part of the foot, you should have less space between the edge of the foot tracing and the paper's edge—you should have more space at the heel. Compare your pattern with the pattern below.

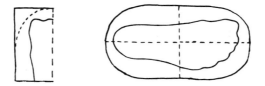

If you think the pattern is too big, refold it and cut off a little more of the paper. Remember to keep the pattern symmetrical, and do not make it narrower at one end. While felting your project it is difficult to keep track of the heel or toe end. Therefore, the end that you want for the heel will be determined after felting.

Because everyone's feet are shaped differently—some wide and some narrow—the pattern you start with is important for achieving custom-fitted footwear. When your paper pattern is finished, trace it onto a piece of cotton fabric, then cut it out. You now have a finished cotton pattern.

Making a Pattern for Boots

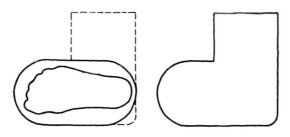

The pattern for the boot is the basic shape shown here. The length, however, is determined by the length of the feet for which you are making it. The pattern may be made taller if you want a higher top on your boot.

To make a boot pattern, follow the instructions for making a slipper pattern, then put your symmetrical paper pattern on another sheet of paper and draw in the ankle extension on the top of one end. Finally, fill in the bottom of the heel as shown.

Making a Pattern for Mittens

Step 1. To make a pattern for a pair of mittens, have the person for whom you are making the mittens rest one arm on a table. Place a piece of paper under the hand and wrist. Be sure the paper extends at least 2 inches around the hand. Have the person keep his or her fingers together and the thumb extended as the person would when wearing a mitten.

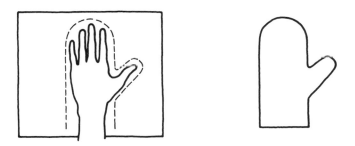

Step 2. Carefully trace around the hand with a pen or pencil, keeping the line even and about three-quarters of an inch away from the hand. Round the top of the mitten around the fingers. Be sure the line is even and approximately the same distance from the hand all around.

Step 3. Cut out the pattern, trace it onto a piece of cotton fabric, then cut out the cotton pattern.

Making a Pattern for a Hat

Hats come in many styles and shapes and are fun to experiment with. The shape of your face or the preference of the person for whom you are making the hat will determine the hat style that you choose to make. The shape of your finished hat depends on your pattern, your wool, and how you shape your hat in the last step of making it. The basic hat pattern is found in Appendix D. If you desire a different shape to your hat, you may make changes to the basic pattern according to the suggestions given.

Basic Hat Pattern

This pattern results in a fedora, a brimmed hat that does not fit snugly to the top of your head. There is a space between the top of the hat and the top of your head which allows you to push in on this part to give a crease in the top of the hat. The brim on this hat is made after the fulling step—you place the hat on a flat surface and let the brim flare out.

Variations on the Basic Hat Pattern

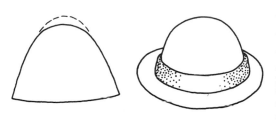

Starting with the basic pattern, the top of the hat is lowered so the hat fits snugly to the top of the head. The bottom of the pattern is the same as the basic hat pattern so that the brim will be even all around the hat. The brim can be made stiffer by steaming it with a hot iron while it is still damp. To make a larger brim on this hat, extend the pattern down. To make a brimless, tight-fitting cap, shorten the height of the pattern by cutting off the brim area.

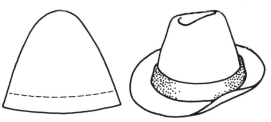

You can extend the basic pattern 2 to 3 inches on the bottom to make a taller fedora with a wider brim, similar to a cowboy hat. This brim may also be shaped by steaming it—when the brim is still wet, iron it with a hot iron, put it on, and shape it. Let it dry in the shape that you like best.

6

The Felting Process

The change in the wool as a result of water, soap, and continuous massage can best be understood by feeling it happen. As a beginning felter, you might be working on the wool while daydreaming and, all of a sudden, you find that the fibers you are working on have suddenly felted! It can be like magic. One moment it was a mass of wet fibers and the next, it was a piece of material. With more experience, however, you will be able to feel the changes that gradually happen in the wool while you work through the felting process. But it can still seem like magic!

The Committee on Textiles of the American Society for Testing and Materials (ASTM) defines felt to be "a textile structure composed entirely of fibers physically interlocked and consolidated by the utilization of mechanical work, chemical action and moisture without the use of weaving, knitting, stitching, thermal bonding or adhesives." The felting process depends on the scaly surface of the individual wool fibers. Because of the arrangement of the scales, the wool fibers can only move easily in one direction along their length. The tendency of wool fibers to shrink when they are exposed to soap, hot water, and continuous massage causes the scales to interlock with those of other fibers. These factors allow a batt of wool fibers to become irreversibly bonded into felt material. The felting process is demonstrated all too well when you accidently put a wool sweater in the washing machine. Wools that shrink the most and fastest, under these conditions, are the best for felting—these wools fall into the fast-felting category.

Stepping Through the Felting Procedure

When making any of the items in this book, you will begin the felting process after your wool is wetted down in the shape of your pattern, with your pattern inside. (You will find the actual instructions for making felt wearables in Chapter 8.)

Step 1. It is important to start slowly by gently pushing the wool down with your fingertips all over the pattern. If the wool sticks to your fingers, you may need more soapy water, or you may be pushing down too hard. Continue this for three to five minutes, depending on the size of your project and the type of wool. Fast-felting wool, for example, will take less time than a slower wool for the same size pattern.

Begin by gently pushing down with your fingertips.

Step 2. The wool will not feel as soft after a while. You may then test it by gently making a circular motion, keeping your fingers flat. If the fibers seem to come loose or move, continue pushing straight down, but use more pressure. Try circular movements again after a few minutes, and gradually use more pressure. If you make your rubbing movements too large or start with circular movements too soon, you may get strings of fibers coming out from the felt in some spots. These can sometimes be felted onto your piece by pushing down on them, but they most likely will have to be cut off when you finish the project. Try to avoid this problem by working more gently and patiently at first.

When the wool stiffens, use more pressure.

Step 3. When you have reached the point where the wool feels like it is harder and you are rubbing with circular movements and exerting more pressure without stretching your piece out of shape, you are ready to cut into it.

After cutting the felt and lifting one side off the pattern, continue to rub the piece all over, exerting as much pressure as you can (follow the directions in Chapter 8 for felting the sides first). The felting procedure for one piece (a slipper or boot, for example) should not take more than 30 to 40 minutes, depending on the type of wool you are using.

Cut into the slipper when the fibers have felted.

Rub the slipper all over using a lot of pressure to harden the felt.

When your wool is felted into solid material, you need to decide whether your project is

- the size you want
- the shape you want
- stiff enough

Depending on what you decide, you may continue rubbing with your hands to

- shrink the item to size
- shape it
- harden the felt by rubbing with your hands (first rinse the piece and squeeze out the water, then add hot, soapy water and rub to smooth and stiffen)

To shrink and harden the felt faster, you may choose to use a washboard or felting board. In that case, you would go on to the fulling step, which is explained in Chapter 7.

7

The Fulling Process

Fulling involves rubbing the wool felt on a washboard, felting board, or similar rough surface to shrink and toughen the material. Different wools shrink at different rates when worked by hand, and they also shrink differently on the washboard. Fast- and medium-felting wools tend to shrink or toughen quickly. This is why it's important not to get carried away with rubbing the felt too long. Thirty seconds may be all that you need to obtain the results you want. Some projects, however, may require five minutes or more of fulling, depending on the amount of shrinkage you wish to obtain. Wool will continue to shrink with continued rubbing—however, as the felt toughens, it will take more and more pressure to obtain more shrinkage. Just as an adult-size slipper can be shrunk to child-size, a very stretched-out slipper may be shrunk back to size by continued fulling.

Stepping Through the Fulling Procedure

Step 1. Rinse out your project and examine it to determine how much it needs to shrink and in what areas. For example, if you are making a pair of slippers for yourself, try them on and check the fit. If they are the correct shape but just too large, you will need to shrink them evenly all over. If the slipper seems to fit in the heel but the length is too long, you may only have to shrink the toe.

Step 2. Dunk your felt project in hot, soapy water and start the fulling process. Work on the material by placing your hand inside your project and rubbing one layer of felt between the washboard and your hand. At first, rub gently to be sure the felt is strong enough to tolerate the rubbing without pulling apart. As the felt toughens and shrinks, rub harder if your project requires more shrinkage. The wool will shrink in the direction that you rub.

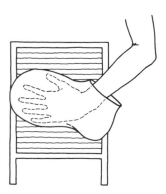

   To shrink the slipper or other item all over, give it a one-eighth to one-quarter turn after every two or three strokes up and down. To shrink the toe or the heel, rub these areas in a circular motion with your hand inside the slipper.

Support the project with one hand when fulling on the washboard.

Shrink the length by rubbing lengthwise.

8
Making Felt Wearables

FELT SLIPPERS

Felt items are very comfortable to wear. The wool is not scratchy after it is felted, and a pair of warm felt slippers feels very cozy on your feet. Felt slippers make you feel like you are walking on a cloud. Making a pair of slippers is a good way to learn to felt. If you can resist making a pair for yourself, it is easier to make a pair for a young child as your first project. Smaller pieces take less time to work on, and they are easier to control. Making an adult-size pair of slippers as your first project may be a little overwhelming.

If this is your first experience making a felt item for wear, keep in mind these two points:

1. Obtain wool which has been shown to be good for felting (see explanation in Chapter 1). You want the wool to felt fairly quickly.

2. Be patient and do not expect immediate results. Until your technique is fully developed it will take you a longer time to get the wool to felt than it would take someone who has more experience (see Chapter 6, The Felting Process).

Making A Pair of Slippers

Step 1. Medium-felting wool is best for making slippers. Blending fast-felting wool with slow-felting wool will give you medium-felting wool. Four to five ounces is usually enough wool for a pair of slippers for an adult, while three ounces is enough for a child's. When making a large pair (men's size), however, you may need to card six ounces or more in order to have about five layers per batt. Because they take more wear from being worn on the feet, the batts should be thicker than when making hats or mittens.

Step 2. Weigh out 4-5 ounces of wool for an adult size or 3 ounces for a child size. Card the wool and weigh out four equal piles of wool—1 to 1¼ ounces each for an adult size or ¾ ounce each for a child size.

Step 3. Make a pattern according to the directions in Chapter 5, or trace a pattern from Appendix D onto a piece of cotton fabric. It is helpful if the cotton for your pattern is a different color than your wool. Lay your pattern on the work surface and, with one-fourth of the carded wool, make your first batt. Use the slipper pattern as your guide (see Making Batts in Chapter 2). Let the wool extend out from the edge of the pattern about 1½ inches. Taper the wool at the edges so it will blend smoothly when you join the two batts together.

The first layer of wool for the batt should be arranged over the pattern. Arrange the next layer as pictured below, and then repeat with the remainder of the pile of wool. If you still have wool left, keep layering it. In each layer, the wool fibers should lie perpendicular to the fibers in the previous layer.

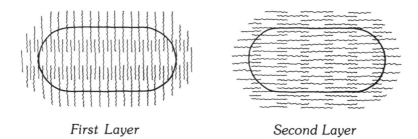

First Layer   Second Layer

Repeat the same process with the remaining three piles of wool. When you finish, you will have four batts of wool.

When making the wool batts, try to keep them as even as possible. Hold them up to the light to see if there are any holes that need more wool. If you card the wool evenly and equally, in addition to weighing the wool separately, you should have even batts. Uneven batts can result in thin spots or holes in your slippers.

Step 4. Before beginning on this step, you will need to have two to three quarts of hot, soapy water ready. Make the water as hot as your hands can stand. If you are working outdoors, you will need a bucket of clear rinse water (hot or cold). If you are working at a sink, you can rinse the slipper under running water.

Lay your first wool batt down on a dry work surface (preferably a wooden table or cutting board). Dampen your pattern in the hot water and center it on top of the batt.

Pull off extra wool at the corners of the batt to make the wool extend out evenly all around the pattern.

Slowly add hot, soapy water, about one-quarter cup at a time, while you push down on the pattern. Thoroughly wet the wool under the pattern, being certain to keep the wool that extends beyond the sides of the pattern dry. When the wool under the whole pattern is wet, push down with your fingertips over the entire pattern for three to five minutes. This will start the felting process under the pattern to hold the wool together when you turn it over in Step 5.

Next, using the dry wool that extends out from the pattern, fold it in over the pattern all around.

Be sure to make the fold right on the edge of the pattern. Bunch the wool up over the pattern, then use soapy water to wet it down on the pattern.

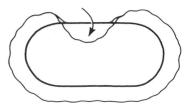

After turning in all of the wool, there may be an area in the center of the slipper where the pattern is not covered. This is more likely with an adult slipper pattern that is wider than three inches. In this case, you may add more carded wool in the area not covered so that the felt will be even.

Add more wool to this area if necessary

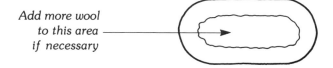

Step 5. Wipe away any standing water around your slipper, then place your second batt of wool over your wet pattern and wool. Press down over the middle of the batt, then add more hot, soapy water to mat the wool onto your pattern. Carefully find the edge of the pattern by pressing down with your fingertips over the second batt. Wet down the wool only to the edge of the pattern, keeping the outside wool dry.

When the wool above the pattern is all wetted down, continue to press gently with your fingertips for three to five minutes to slightly felt the wool.

Now pick up the slipper at the end farthest away from you and flip the whole thing over. Fold the dry wool over the pattern on this back side while you wet it down with more soapy water. Again, be sure to make the fold right on the edge of the pattern.

At this point you have wet wool that is lying in the shape of a slipper, but the fibers are not felted and can easily be pulled apart. Now you are ready to felt the wool, hardening it to form material that stays together. You will then cut into the top and open up the slipper.

Step 6. Begin felting the wool by gently pushing down with your fingertips all over the slipper. Avoid working at the edge of the slipper, because you may get a thick rolled area all around the sides. You may also change the shape of the slipper. As you massage and work on the wool, keep the piece in the same shape as your pattern. Don't push down too hard at the beginning or the slipper may get too large.

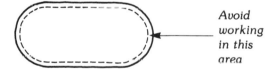

Avoid working in this area

As you feel the fibers begin to cling together and not move too much when you press down, you can use more pressure. Eventually, you will be working on the piece in a circular motion with your whole hand. If the fibers stick to your hands when you lift your hands off the wool, you are either using too much pressure or you need to add more hot, soapy water.

When you turn the slipper over, you must start the felting process all over again. Begin by gently pushing down with your fingertips. During this process, continue to add hot, soapy water as it is needed. If your slipper becomes too sudsy, immerse it in a pan of hot or cold water, gently squeeze it out, then add more hot, soapy water and continue to massage. (Too many suds will cause soap bubbles to fill up the spaces between the wool fibers, preventing them from coming in contact with each other.) This felting process may take 10 to 15 minutes or longer, depending on the type of wool you are using.

After finishing this step, immerse the slipper in clear water and gently squeeze it out. Be careful not to pull the edge wool when you squeeze it. The slipper should hold together pretty well.

Step 7. Now you are ready to open up your slipper. Pick the best side to be the top, and decide which end you want for the toe. Lay the slipper flat on the work surface. With a pair of pointed scissors, cut in from the top until you locate the pattern. This is easier if your pattern is a different color than your wool. Try not to cut into the pattern.

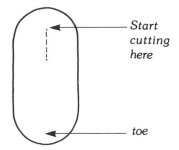

Start cutting here

toe

Put your finger in the hole and lift the top wool away from the pattern. If you are making an adult slipper, start cutting 1½ to 2 inches in from the heel and cut a slit that is the same width as the four knuckles on your hand. For a child's slipper start cutting 1 to 1½ inches in from the heel.

Fit your hand into the slipper to work on the inside. With the fingers of both hands, felt the opening you just cut to stiffen this area so it won't stretch out of shape.

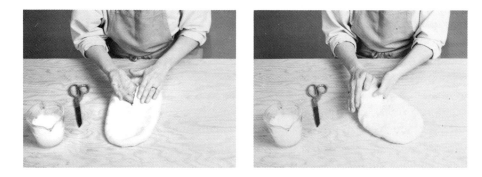

Next, with one hand supporting the edge area on the inside, push in all around the edge that you avoided previously. Work on the heel area first, pushing with your outside hand against the hand inside the slipper. Felt and shape the heel, rubbing with upward strokes to bring the heel higher.

Rub with an upward movement while pressing together.

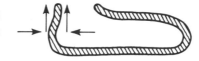

Cross Section of Slipper

Start with small movements and gradually felt and smooth out the edge area or seam before working on the rest of the slipper. Continue to massage the slipper all over, inside and outside, by rubbing with your hands in a circular motion. Use as much pressure as you can. Remove the pattern and massage the wool that was under the pattern.

Now you should have a large slipper that holds together but will not necessarily hold the shape. If you started with fast-felting wool, however, this may not be the case. If your slipper is the correct size now, do not go on to Step 8, the fulling step, or your slipper will shrink too much. If the slipper is too big, you can shrink and shape it as described in the next step.

Step 8. If your project needs it, you are now ready to begin the fulling process, in which you shrink and shape your slipper (see Chapter 7 for a complete description of the fulling process). Rub your slipper on a washboard. The wool will shrink in the direction that you rub. If the slipper is much too big, rub it all around the outside in order to bring the sides in. Rub the toe in a circular motion to shrink it. Stop frequently and check how your slipper is shaping up, then continue to rub where you want it to shrink. After completing this step, your slipper will be smaller and stiffer. If it is not small enough, keep rubbing it all over on the washboard. You may also shrink and shape the slipper at this point by putting it on your foot or on the foot of the person it is for and rubbing it with your hands.

Step 9. Your slipper should be the shape and size that you want after you finish the fulling process. Use the paper foot tracing to check the size. Then cut around the opening to smooth it out or to make the opening large enough to get the foot in. After cutting, add more hot, soapy water and rub the cut edges.

For the second slipper, repeat the same steps with your other two batts of wool. Use your finished slipper as a guide for size when making the second one.

When you have made both slippers, rinse them and squeeze them out. It is not necessary to get every last bit of soap out. Shape your slippers by standing them on the table and pulling the top up, or try them on and set them down to dry in the same shape. After they dry, the slippers are ready to be decorated.

Slippers that are too small will stretch a little while they are still wet, but if they are still too small, you need to find a smaller person to give them to. If you followed the instructions carefully for making a pattern, the problem may be that your wool felted too quickly. You can try mixing it with some wool that will not turn to felt so fast. Your slipper may also have gotten too small if you overdid it when fulling your project on the washboard. The wool sometimes shrinks very quickly, and just a few rubs may be enough to shrink a certain area.

FELT BOOTS

Felt boots make warm slippers for people who live in cold climates. They also make nice après-ski boots. Boots will keep your feet and ankles warm. You can extend the top to cover more of your lower leg.

Making A Pair of Boots

Step 1. Use medium-felting wool or blend fast-felting wool with slow-felting wool to give you more control over the shrinkage of the boot. At least six ounces of carded wool is needed for an adult pair. Each batt should have at least five layers.

Make a pattern according to the directions in Chapter 5, or trace a pattern from Appendix D onto a piece of cotton fabric. It is helpful if the cotton for your pattern is a different color than your wool.

Step 2. Separate your wool into four equal piles. Card each pile separately, or weigh the wool into equal parts after carding.

Step 3. Lay your pattern on your work surface and, with one-fourth of the carded wool, make your first batt. Use the boot pattern as your guide (see Making Batts in Chapter 2). Let the wool extend out from the the edge of the pattern about 1½ inches. Taper the wool at the edges so it will blend smoothly when you join the two batts together.

The first layer of wool for the batt should be arranged over the pattern. Arrange the next layer as shown below. Continue the alternating pattern for the third, fourth, and fifth layers. If you still have wool left, keep layering it alternately. In each layer, the wool fibers should lie perpendicular to the fibers in the previous layer.

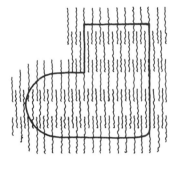

First Layer

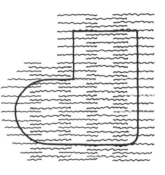

Second Layer

Step 4. Before beginning on the next step, have two to three quarts of hot, soapy water ready. Depending on the size of the boots you are making, you may want to work outdoors. Carefully lay your first wool batt down on your work surface, preferably a wooden table or cutting board to prevent the wool from sliding. Dampen your pattern and center it on top of the  batt. Slowly add hot, soapy water, about ⅛ cup at a time, while you push down on the pattern. Thoroughly wet only the wool under the pattern, being certain to keep the wool that extends beyond the sides of the pattern dry. When the wool under the whole pattern is wet, push down over the entire pattern for three to five minutes. This will start the felting process under the pattern to hold the wool together when you turn it over in Step 5.

Next, using the dry wool that extends out from the pattern, fold it in over the pattern all around. Be sure to make the fold right on the edge of the pattern.

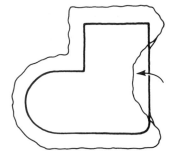

Pull the batting apart at the curved part of the boot to make the wool lie flatter when it is folded over.

Bunch the wool up over the pattern, then use hot, soapy water to wet it down on the pattern. Add more wool to the middle of the pattern if it is not covered. Wipe up any water around the boot before going to Step 5.

Step 5. Next, center your second batt of wool over your wet pattern. Press down over the middle of the batt, then add more hot, soapy water to mat the wool onto your pattern. Carefully find the edge of the pattern by pressing down with your fingertips over the second batt. Wet down the wool only to the edge of the pattern, keeping the outside wool dry.

When the wool above the pattern is all wetted down, continue to press gently with your fingertips for five minutes to slightly felt the wool. Then pick up the boot at the top of the pattern and flip the whole thing over. Fold the dry wool over the pattern on this back side while you wet it down with more water.

Step 6. At this point you have wet wool that is lying in the shape of a boot, but the fibers do not cling together and can be easily pulled apart. Now you are ready to felt the wool, hardening it to form material that holds together. Then you will cut into the top and open up the boot.

Begin felting the wool by gently pushing down with your fingertips all over the boot. Avoid working at the edge of the boot, because you may get a thick roll on the side or stretch the boot out of shape.

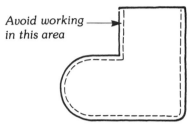

Avoid working in this area

As you feel the fibers start to cling together and not move too much when you touch them, you can use more pressure. If the wool sticks to your hands as you lift them off the boot, you either need more hot, soapy water or you need to use less pressure. Eventually, you will be working on the boot in a circular motion with your whole hand, using a lot of pressure.

When you turn the boot over, you must start the felting process over again. Begin by gently pushing down with your fingertips. During this process, continue to add hot, soapy water when needed. If your boot becomes too sudsy, immerse it in a pail of clear water (hot or cold), gently squeeze it out, and then continue the massage. The felting process may take 15 to 20 minutes or longer, depending on the type of wool you are using.

After finishing this step, immerse your boot in clear water and gently squeeze it out. Be careful not to pull the edge wool when squeezing. There should be no dirty water coming out of the boot, and it should hold together pretty well.

Step 7. Lay your boot flat on the work surface. With a pair of pointed scissors, cut in from the top end of the boot until you locate the pattern (see figure on next page). This is easier if your pattern is a different color than your wool.

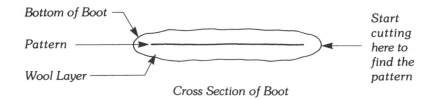

Bottom of Boot
Pattern
Wool Layer

Start cutting here to find the pattern

Cross Section of Boot

Put your finger in the hole in order to lift the wool up off the pattern, then cut sideways to make an opening all along the top of your boot.

Place one hand inside the boot and pull the top side away from the pattern. Leave the pattern in the boot clinging to the other side in order to give it support while you continue to felt. First felt the edge area of the boot that you avoided in the previous step. With one hand supporting the edge area inside the boot, push down from the outside with your other hand all along the edge. Start with small movements and gradually make firm circular movements to smooth out the edge area and toughen it before working on the rest of the boot. Continue to felt the boot all over, inside and outside, by rubbing with your hands in a circular motion. Remove the pattern and massage the wool that was under the pattern.

Now you should have a large boot that holds together, is not stiff, and is tough enough for wear. If the boot is too big for your foot, shrink it on the washboard or put it on and rub it while you are wearing it. If the boot has shrunk enough at this point, Step 8 will make it too small, so go on to Step 9.

Step 8. If your project needs it, you are now ready to begin the fulling process, in which you shrink and shape your boot (see Chapter 7 for a complete description of the fulling process). If the boot seems much too big, rub it on a washboard all around the outside. The wool will shrink in the direction that you rub. Check the size every half minute or so to be sure you don't shrink it too much.

Some wools will shrink very quickly during this process, while other wools will not. If the foot is too long, rub the toe in a circular motion to shrink it, and rub the whole boot lengthwise.

After completing this step, your boot should be stiffer and smaller and ready to be shaped. The boot lends itself to being shaped on the foot. Put it on to determine where more shrinkage or shaping is needed.

Step 9. For an even opening on the top of the boot, cut the felt with a pair of sharp scissors and then felt the cut edges by adding hot, soapy water and rubbing them until they hold together. After each boot is finished, put it on to shape it and then take it off and let it dry in the shape of your foot.

Follow the same procedure for your second boot. Use the finished boot as a guide for size as you shrink and shape your second one.

FELT MITTENS

Felt mittens look very unique when you wear them, like the other felt items you can make. Embroidering them with colorful wool yarn shows them off. The mittens are made with a thinner felt, so when you start, your batts will be thinner. It is important to have enough wool at the angle between the thumb and the fingers because this area receives the most wear, so add extra wool here for reinforcement.

Making a Pair of Mittens

Step 1. To make a pair of mittens, choose medium-felting wool. Two and a half ounces of wool is sufficient for an adult pair of mittens, while 1½ to 2 ounces is enough for a child's pair.

Step 2. Make a pattern according to the directions in Chapter 5, or use the pattern from Appendix D traced onto a piece of cotton fabric. It is helpful if your pattern is a different color than your wool.

Step 3. Lay your pattern on your work surface and, with one-fourth of the carded wool, make your first batt. Use the mitten pattern as a guide (see Making Batts in Chapter 2). Let the wool extend out from the edge of the pattern about 1½ inches. Taper the wool at the edges so it will blend in smoothly when you join the two batts together.

The first layer of wool should be arranged over the pattern. Arrange the second layer as shown below, then repeat with the third and fourth layers. If you still have wool left, keep layering it alternately. In each layer, the wool fibers should lie perpendicular to the fibers in the previous layer.

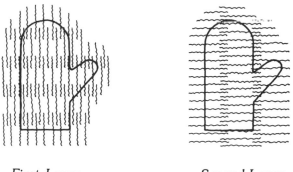

First Layer   Second Layer

Before beginning on the next step, you will need to have two to three quarts of hot, soapy water ready. If you are not working at a sink, you will need a pan of clear water for rinsing.

Step 4. Lay your first wool batt down on the work surface (preferably a wooden table or cutting board). Dampen your pattern and center it on top of the batt. Slowly add hot, soapy water, about ⅛ cup at a time, while you push down on the pattern. Thoroughly wet the wool under the pattern, being sure to keep the wool that extends beyond the sides of the pattern dry. When the wool under the whole pattern is wetted down, push down over the entire pattern for about three to five minutes with your fingertips. This will start the felting

process under the pattern and hold the wool together when you turn the mitten over in Step 5.

Next, using the dry wool that extends out from the pattern, fold it in over the pattern all around. Be sure to make the fold right on the edge of the pattern. Bunch the wool up over the pattern, then use hot, soapy water to wet it down on the pattern. Add more wool to the middle of the pattern if it is not covered. Wipe up any water around the mitten before going on to Step 5.

Add extra wool to the area between the thumb and fingers because this area gets the most wear.

Step 5. Center your second batt of wool over your pattern. Press down over the middle of the batt, then add more hot, soapy water to mat the wool onto your pattern. Carefully find the edge of the pattern by pressing down with your fingertips over the second batt. Wet down the wool only to the edge of the pattern, keeping the outside wool dry.

When the wool above the pattern is all wetted down, continue to press gently with your fingertips for three to five minutes to slightly felt the wool. Then, pick up the mitten at the top of the pattern and flip the whole thing over.

Fold the dry wool over the pattern on this side while you wet it down with more hot, soapy water.

Add more wool to the center of the mitten on the other side if necessary.

Step 6. At this point you have wet wool that is lying in the shape of a mitten, but the fibers do not cling together and can be easily pulled apart. Now you are ready to felt the wool, hardening it to form material that holds together. You will then cut into the bottom and open up the mitten.

Begin felting the wool by gently pushing down with your fingertips all over the mitten. Avoid working at the edge of the mitten, because you may get a thick, rolled area all around the sides.

Avoid working in this area →

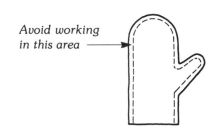

As you feel the fibers start to cling together and the wool become firmer, then you can use more pressure. Eventually, you will be working on the piece in a circular motion with your whole hand.

When you turn the mitten over, you must start the felting process over again. Begin by gently pushing down with your fingertips. During this process, continue to add hot, soapy water when needed. If your mitten becomes too sudsy, immerse it in a pail of clear water (hot or cold) and gently squeeze it out. Then go back to your work area, add more hot, soapy water, and continue the massage. The felting process may take 10 to 15 minutes or longer, depending on the type of wool you are using.

After finishing this step, immerse your mitten in clear water and gently squeeze it out. Be careful not to pull the edge wool when squeezing.

Step 7. Lay your mitten flat on your work surface. With a pair of pointed scissors, cut in from the bottom until you locate the pattern. This is easier if the pattern is a different color than your wool.

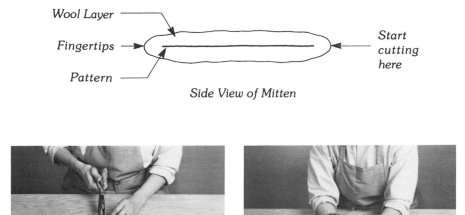

Wool Layer

Fingertips →

Pattern →

Start cutting here ←

Side View of Mitten

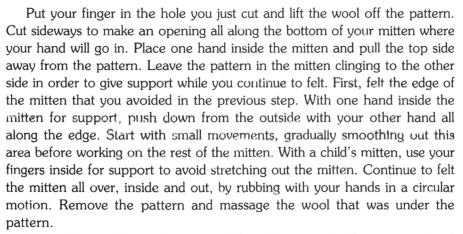

Put your finger in the hole you just cut and lift the wool off the pattern. Cut sideways to make an opening all along the bottom of your mitten where your hand will go in. Place one hand inside the mitten and pull the top side away from the pattern. Leave the pattern in the mitten clinging to the other side in order to give support while you continue to felt. First, felt the edge of the mitten that you avoided in the previous step. With one hand inside the mitten for support, push down from the outside with your other hand all along the edge. Start with small movements, gradually smoothing out this area before working on the rest of the mitten. With a child's mitten, use your fingers inside for support to avoid stretching out the mitten. Continue to felt the mitten all over, inside and out, by rubbing with your hands in a circular motion. Remove the pattern and massage the wool that was under the pattern.

Depending on the wool you used, the mitten may be the correct size at this point. If this is so, rinse it out and follow the same procedure for the second mitten, using the first one as a guide for size. If the mitten is too big and you want to shrink it further, either continue rubbing it with your hands or use the washboard for fulling (see Step 8).

Step 8. If your mitten needs it, you are now ready to begin the fulling process, in which you shrink and shape your mittens (see Chapter 7 for a complete description of the fulling process). Using a washboard or felting board, rub the mitten all around the outside. Start slowly and gently to gradually toughen the felt. After the felt is stronger, you can rub harder to shrink the mitten. The wool will shrink in the direction that you rub. To shrink the mitten to size, start with the finger area. Rub all around until that area has shrunk to the correct size, then rub the thumb area until you have shrunk it. Work on the wrist area last. Check the size and shape often (after every five rubs or so) because some wools will shrink very quickly.

Step 9. Your mitten should be the size and shape you want after the fulling process. For an even opening at the wrist, cut the felt with a pair of sharp scissors. Felt the cut edges by adding hot, soapy water and rubbing them until they hold together. Follow the same procedure for the second mitten using the first mitten as a guide.

Rub lengthwise to shrink the length.

FELT HATS

Hats are a lot of fun to make and shape into whatever style or form you like. For a beginner who has not felted before, I suggest felting a small pair of slippers before trying a hat. Although your finished product is only one piece, when making a hat you are working with a larger piece that is harder to control through the felting process.

When making a hat, there are a couple of things to keep in mind. First, to have an even felt, be sure to taper the edges of your batts and to add more carded wool to the area of the pattern that is not covered. Second, remember that the shaping of the hat comes at the end of the process. After a few tries, and looking at the sample patterns in Chapter 5, you will be able to see how to change your pattern if you have an idea that cannot be achieved with the basic pattern.

Making a Hat

For making a hat, choose wool that felts quickly. Fast-felting wool allows you to control the shape more easily. Three ounces of wool is enough for a woman's hat with a brim if you follow the basic pattern in this book. When making a man's hat, you may need an extra one-half ounce of wool in order to have enough for the brim.

Step 1. Make a pattern according to the directions in Chapter 5. Trace the basic pattern from Appendix D onto a piece of paper, then adjust it according to the style you choose. Cut out the adjusted pattern and trace it onto a piece of cotton fabric. It is helpful if your pattern is a different color than your wool.

Step 2. Separate your wool into two equal piles. Card each pile separately, or weigh the wool after carding.

Step 3. Lay your pattern on the work surface and, with one-quarter of the carded wool, make your first batt. Use the pattern as your guide (see Making Batts in Chapter 2). Let the wool extend out 2 to 3 inches from the edge of the pattern. Taper the wool at the edges so it will blend in smoothly when you join the two batts together.

    The first layer of your batt is arranged over the pattern. Arrange the second layer as shown below, and then repeat with the third and fourth layers. If you still have wool left, keep layering it alternately. In each layer, the wool fibers should lie perpendicular to the fibers in the previous layer.

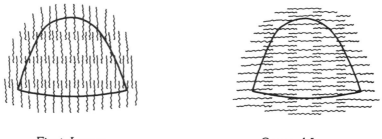

First Layer   *Second Layer*

Step 4. Before beginning on this step, you will need to have two to three quarts of hot, soapy water ready. You will also need a pan of clear water for rinsing. Because of the size of the project, it may be easier to work outdoors.

Lay the first wool batt down on your work surface (preferably a wooden table or cutting board). Dampen your pattern and center it on top of the batt. Slowly add hot, soapy water, about 1/8 cup at a time, while you push down on the pattern. Thoroughly wet the wool under the pattern, being certain to keep the wool that extends beyond the sides of the pattern dry.

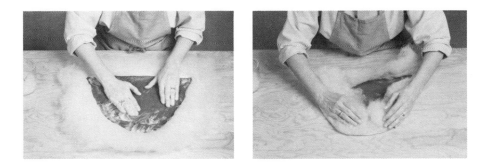

When the wool under the whole pattern is wetted down, push down over the entire pattern for about five minutes. This will start the felting process under the pattern and help hold the wool together when you turn the hat over in Step 5.

Next, using the dry wool that extends out from the pattern, fold it in over the pattern all around. Be sure to make the fold right on the edge of the pattern.

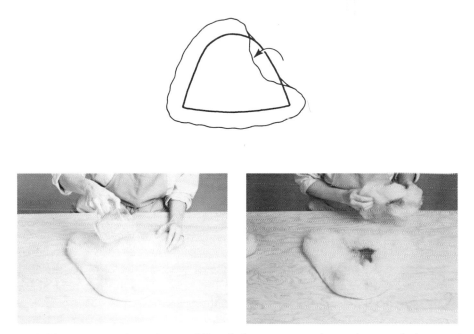

Add more wool to the middle of the pattern where the wool does not cover. One to two thin layers will help make the felt more even.

Use hot, soapy water to mat the dry wool down on the pattern.

For a thicker brim, add an extra row of wool at the bottom of the hat.

Wet down the wool lying over the pattern and keep the wool dry that extends past the edge. Dry the work area around your hat before going to Step 5.

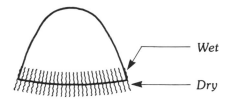

Wet

Dry

Step 5. Center your second batt of wool over your pattern. Press down over the middle of the batt, then add more hot, soapy water to mat the wool onto your pattern. Carefully find the edge of the pattern by pressing down with your fingertips over the second batt. Wet down the wool only to the edge of the pattern, keeping the outside wool dry.

When the wool above the pattern is all wetted down, continue to press gently with your fingertips for three to five minutes to slightly felt the wool. Now pick up the hat at the top of the pattern and flip the whole thing over. Fold the dry wool over the pattern on this back side while you wet it down with more hot, soapy water. Add more wool to the center area if you did so on the first side. If you added an extra row of wool to the brim on the first side, repeat the same procedure now on this side. Turn the hat over again and fold the dry wool over the wet wool at the brim.

Step 6. At this point you have wet wool that is in the shape of a hat, but the wool does not cling together and the fibers can be easily pulled apart. Now you are ready to felt the wool and harden the material enough to cut into the bottom and open up the hat.

Begin felting the wool by gently pushing down with your fingertips all over the hat. Avoid working at the edge of the hat, because you may get a thick, rolled area around the edge.

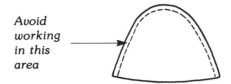

Avoid working in this area

As you feel the fibers start to cling together and not move too much when you touch them, you can use more pressure. Eventually, you will be working on the piece in a circular motion with your whole hand.

When you turn the hat over, you must start the felting process over again. Begin by gently pushing down with your fingertips. During the felting process, continue to add hot, soapy water when needed. If the hat becomes too sudsy, immerse it in a pan of clear water (hot or cold) and gently squeeze it out. Then go back to your work area—add more hot, soapy water and continue the massage. This felting process may take 15 to 20 minutes or longer, depending on the type of wool you are using.

After finishing this step, immerse your hat in clear water and gently squeeze it out. The fibers should be holding together pretty well. Be careful not to pull the edge wool when squeezing.

Step 7. Lay your hat flat on your work surface. With a pair of pointed scissors, cut in from the bottom of the hat until you locate the pattern. This is easier if your pattern is a different color than your wool.

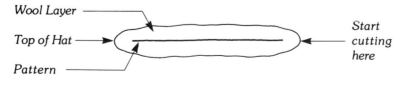

Wool Layer

Top of Hat

Pattern

Start cutting here

Cross Section of Hat

Put your finger in the hole in order to lift the top wool up away from the pattern. Cut sideways to make an opening all along the bottom of your hat. Do not cut up at the corners.

Place one hand inside the hat and pull the top side away from the pattern. Leave the pattern in the hat clinging to the other side in order to give it support while you continue to felt. First felt the edge area of the hat that you avoided in the previous step. With one hand supporting the edge area inside the hat, push in from the outside with your other hand all along the edge. Start with small movements and gradually felt and smooth out the edge area before working on the rest of the hat. Continue to massage the hat all over, inside and outside, by rubbing with your hands in a circular motion. Remove the pattern and massage the wool that was under the pattern.

Now you should have a large, cone-shaped hat that holds together but will not hold any shape. Most likely, the hat is too big for your head, so next, you will shrink and harden the felt so that you can form it into the shape that you want. This process, called fulling, is described in the next step.

Step 8. Hold the hat sideways and rub it against the washboard all around the middle section (see Figure 8-1). The wool will shrink in the direction that you rub. Rub the top in a circular motion to toughen the material. After completing this step, your hat should be stiffer and narrower. At this point, stand it on a table with the brim flaring out (see Figure 8-2).

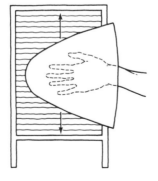

Figure 8-1

Figure 8-2

Step 9. First stiffen the brim by adding more hot, soapy water and rubbing it while pushing down. Rinse out the hat and try it on.

Check where you want the hat to be shrunk more and then, by rubbing with your hands or using the washboard, you can shrink or smooth different areas of your hat. Continue to felt, rinse, and try the hat on until you have obtained the shape you want.

After you have the shape that you want, cut the brim to make it more symmetrical. Finish off the cut edge by rubbing it after adding hot, soapy water.

You do not have to get every last bit of soap out of the hat. To rinse it, pour water over the hat until most of the soap runs out. The water drains out of the hat fairly quickly without squeezing. Wringing the hat can change the shape and shrink it.

After the hat is rinsed out, you may use your iron (on wool setting) to steam the brim. Place a towel on your ironing board and iron the damp brim. Be careful not to scorch the wool. After you have steamed the brim, put the hat on and shape the brim. Set the hat down and let it dry in the shape that you desire.

Decorating Your Hat

Decorating your hat is even more fun. You can change the character or look of the hat depending on the kinds of decorations that you choose:

Woven bands

Feathers and beads

Embroidery

Dyeing

Sewing machine stitching with contrasting colors

9
More Felt Items to Make

After you feel confident with the wool you are using and the felting technique, you may wish to invent your own felt article or make other felt items. Wall hangings, purses, toys, rugs, vests, and many other things can be made from felt with the same technique—using hot, soapy water and continuous manipulation. The following are a few ideas that you may elaborate on.

BERET

A felt beret is easier to make than a fedora or hat using the basic hat pattern. The beret uses a circle pattern and does not require shaping.

Making a Beret

Step 1. Trace a pattern onto a piece of cloth using a large round platter as your guide. Cut out your pattern.

Step 2. With 2 to 2½ ounces of carded wool, make two batts. Let the wool extend 3 to 4 inches out from your pattern.

Step 3. Follow the same steps as with the hat instructions until you have the pattern enveloped between the two batts. If the wool is too thin in the middle after folding it over the pattern, add more wool to cover the pattern.

Wet down the wool under the pattern.

Fold the wool over the pattern starting at the edge of the pattern.

Add wool to the middle to cover the pattern.

Step 4. Begin felting the beret until the felt is strong enough to cut into.

Step 5. Cut a slit in the center of the beret, large enough to fit your hand. Felt the cut edge, then work the outside edge of the beret first. Continue to felt the beret, inside and out.

Step 6. When the felt is strong enough, begin the fulling process of shrinking it evenly on the washboard.

Step 7. After the beret has shrunk to the size you want and the felt is the toughness that you desire, cut a hole around the slit. Start with a small hole, try the beret on, then make it larger if necessary. Felt the cut edge with hot, soapy water.

Step 8. When the beret is dry, sewing a piece of suede or soft material around the cut edge is a nice finish.

PURSE OR HANDBAG

A small- to medium-size purse or handbag can be made using the same seamless technique. The pattern is a piece of cotton as big as you want the purse to be, plus enough for the flap. The technique for making the body of the purse is the same as for slippers or any other item that is open on the inside. The flap is made by folding the dry wool over onto the wet wool. In this way, the pattern is used as a guide rather than being enveloped by the wool.

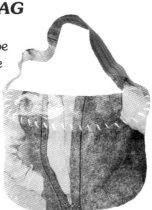

Making a Purse or Handbag

Step 1. Cut out a piece of cloth one inch larger all around than the size you want the purse, plus enough for the flap. With a pen or permanent marker, draw a line on the pattern to serve as a guide to indicate where the flap starts. The shrinkage will vary with the wool used, so make the pattern larger or smaller according to your wool.

Step 2. Using 2 to 4 ounces of carded wool (depending on the size of the purse), make three batts as shown. Batt 1 uses a little less than half of the total amount of wool—divide the remaining wool between Batts 2 and 3 according to how big the flap is (for example, two thirds for the body and one third for the flap.) There should be at least four layers to each batt.

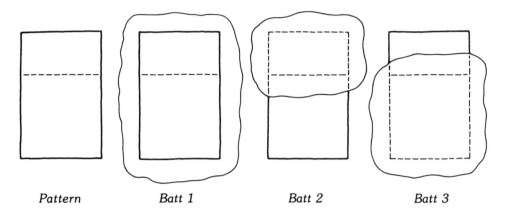

| Pattern | Batt 1 | Batt 2 | Batt 3 |

Step 3. Place the largest batt (Batt 1) down on your work surface and center your wet pattern on top of it. Add hot, soapy water to wet down the wool under the pattern.

Step 4. Using the dry wool that extends out beyond the pattern, fold the dry wool over the pattern of the body of the purse. Fold the dry wool under the pattern for the flap area. Wet the wool down.

Step 5. Place Batt 2 over the body of the purse and wet it down over the pattern. Fold the dry wool at the opening of the purse *onto* itself *over* the pattern.

Step 6. Lift up the pattern flap and place Batt 3 over the flap area. Lay the pattern over the dry wool, and wet the wool under the pattern again.

Step 7. Flip the purse over and fold the dry wool over onto the wet wool. If you want to use some dyed wool, place it on the dry wool at this stage before wetting it down.

Step 8. Begin to felt the purse all over, inside and out, until the material is strong enough to be rubbed on the washboard.

Step 9. When the purse is the desired size and shape, set it aside to dry.

WALL HANGINGS AND RUGS

A large flat piece of felt (not bigger than 3 by 4 feet) can be made by hand. Because of the large area to be felted, the size and thickness of the piece is limited. Larger and thicker pieces, such as rugs, are rolled in a stiff material and worked on by rolling with the hands or feet while exerting downward pressure. A thinner piece suitable for a wall hanging can be easily made by hand. The large surface area makes it impractical to do most of the manipulation of the fiber by working on only one felt layer at a time. However, by rolling the wool in a piece of cloth, pressure can be exerted on more of the wool at the same time.

Making a Large Flat Piece of Felt

Step 1. Using medium- to fast-felting wool, lay out a large batt (3 by 4 feet) that is at least 6 to 10 layers thick.

Step 2. If you are using dyed wool for your design, follow the directions in Chapter 10 for incorporating dyed wool into your project. If you are using dyed wool, you must first lay out the dyed wool on a large sheet of fabric.

Step 3. Place your batt on a fabric sheet—or on top of the design, if you're using one—and wet the wool down leaving 4 to 5 inches on the sides dry.

Step 4. Lift one side of the fabric sheet and use it to push the dry wool over onto the wet wool. This will give a straight edge to the sides of your project. You may choose to fold the dry wool over with your hands instead. Do the same on all sides for a square or rectangular piece.

Step 5. Fold the fabric sheet over the wool on one side, being sure to make the fold right at the edge of the wool. Starting at the folded edge, slowly roll up the wet wool. The sheet keeps the wool separated as you roll it. When you have finished rolling it up, tie the roll in three places with string.

Step 6. Pour hot, soapy water over the rolled up wool, then squeeze it all over with your hands for about 10 minutes. Continue to add hot, soapy water throughout the process. After about 10 minutes, unroll the wool and roll it up from the edge which is at right angles to the first edge. Be sure to fold the sheet over the edge before rolling it up so two layers of felt are not lying next to each other.

Step 7. Follow the process in Step 6 until the wool starts to harden or turn to felt. Unroll the project and work with your hands on areas that need more felting. Rub the wool on a washboard to further toughen it. Rubbing on the washboard may shrink the piece unevenly, making the sides uneven, but you can cut the edges later to even them out.

VEST

A felt vest is a more difficult item to make. Because of its size, it takes at least twice as long to finish as any of the other projects in this book. Before making a vest, first try several smaller items in order to gain experience with the felting technique. For the vest, choose wool whose felting quality is medium-fast to fast.

A vest can be made one of two ways when using the pattern described below. The first way (vest A) is to envelop the pattern in the wool as when making slippers. In this case you will cut an opening in the front of the vest when you are finished. The second way (vest B) is to attach the two front sections of the vest separately. This technique allows you to make a vest that has more material in the front and can therefore be buttoned or clasped in front.

Making a Vest

Step 1. Choosing Wool: Before starting the project, be sure you have wool that has been tested for felting. Because of the size of the project, medium-fast to fast-felting wool works best. From your experience with the shrink-age of the wool, allow enough leeway with the size of your pattern. Remember, if the vest is too big, you can shrink it to size.

Amount of Wool to Use: The amount of wool needed for a vest depends on the size of the pattern. Fast-felting wool needs a larger pattern, while medium-felting wool needs a smaller pattern. You need five or six layers of wool for each batt, including enough to extend out from the sides of the pat-tern's edge. A woman's size 8 or 10 vest takes about 10 to 12 ounces of carded wool. Weigh your first (large) batt and use an equal amount of wool for the second batt for vest A. Use two-thirds the amount of wool of the large batt for each front batt of vest B.

Step 2. Making Your Pattern: When making a vest, a plastic pattern is preferred. Use a large piece of plastic (for example, use a garbage can liner) and follow the instructions below for making a pattern. The final shape of the pattern is shown in Figure 9-1.

Pattern: Measure the distance from the top of one shoulder to the top of the other shoulder using a tape measure. Hold the tape next to your back so the distance across your back is included in the measurement. Next measure the distance from your neck to your waist. Add one or two inches on each side of the pattern depending on the felting quality of your wool (for fast-felting wool, add 2 inches—for medium-felting wool, add 1 inch). Using these measurements, make a square or rectangular pattern. Remember to cut up at the neck and out at the arm holes, as shown in Figure 9-1. For vest B, which buttons in the front, cut a second piece of plastic the size of your pattern but without the arm and neck extensions.

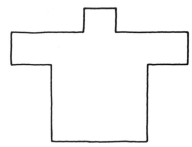

Figure 9-1

Step 3. Making Batts: Even batts are important so you do not end up with holes or very thin spots in the felt. This is especially important when making a vest, because the fabric is mostly made from one batt, except in areas of overlap. Follow the instructions below for making batts, depending on whether you are making vest A or vest B.

Vest A:

Make two batts of equal weight, each five to six layers thick. Extend the wool 5 to 6 inches out from the edges of the pattern. Hold the batts up to the light to check for thin areas—fill these as necessary.

Vest B:

Vest Back: Make one batt using the pattern as a guide. The batt should be five to six layers thick and the wool should extend 5 to 6 inches out from the edges of the pattern.

Vest Front: Make two batts of equal size for the front of the vest. Each "front" batt should be about two-thirds the weight of the "back" batt. When layering the second two batts, use half of the pattern as your guide. If you want the vest to overlap in the front, make each batt using more than half of the pattern as your guide. Let the wool extend 5 to 6 inches out from the edge all around the pattern. Taper the edges of your batts so the felt is not thicker at the seams (see Figure 9-2).

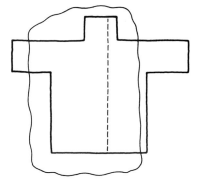

Figure 9-2

Step 4. Wetting down the wool: Place the large batt on your work surface. Center your pattern over the batt. Using hot, soapy water, wet down the wool only under the square part of the pattern (see Figure 9-3). Do not wet the wool under the arm and neck extensions. Next fold the dry wool under the pattern onto the wet wool at the neck and arm hole areas (Figure 9-4). Follow the diagrams for vest A if you are only using two batts or for vest B if you are using three batts.

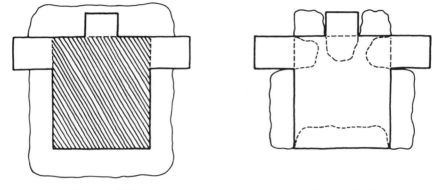

Figure 9-3   Figure 9-4

Vest A:

Fold the dry wool that extends out from the pattern over the pattern. Wet it down (Figure 9-5). Now place the second batt over the pattern and wet down the wool over the rectangular pattern. Be sure to wet only the wool over the pattern, keeping any wool dry that extends past the pattern (Figure 9-6).

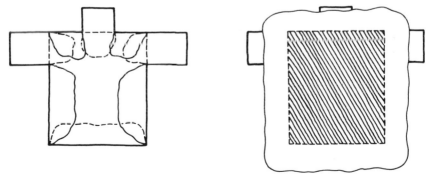

Figure 9-5   Figure 9-6

Now turn the wool under the pattern as in Figures 9-4 and 9-5 but working in the opposite direction. Lift one side of the vest at a time to fold the dry wool under the vest.

Now you have the wool in the position for a vest and it is ready to be felted into a strong material (Figure 9-7). Start the felting process by working one area at a time. When the wool starts to harden, go on to another area until you have covered the front of the vest. Now go to Step 5, Felting.

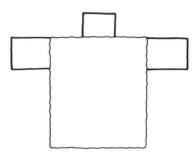

Figure 9-7

Vest B:

Starting at Figure 9-4, fold the dry wool over the pattern on one side only (Figure 9-8), then place one of the smaller batts centered over the same side of the pattern (Figure 9-9). Wet down the wool over half (or 2 to 3 inches more than half) of the pattern, leaving 2 to 3 inches of dry wool over the pattern.

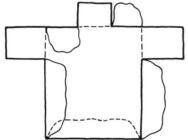

Figure 9-8

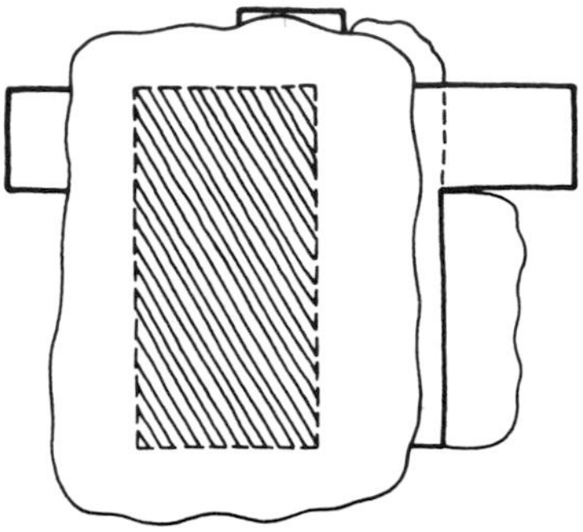

Figure 9-9

Fold the dry wool back onto the wet wool. At the armhole, fold the dry wool under and onto the wet wool. At the shoulder, fold the dry wool over onto the back of the vest. At the waist, fold the dry wool over onto the wet wool where you want the bottom of the vest (see Figure 9-10). When you are finished, your vest should resemble Figure 9-11.

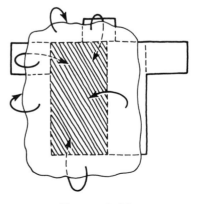

Figure 9-10

Lay your plastic square over the front of the vest to separate the wool that you have already wet down. Then repeat the same steps with the other side. When you have completed the second side, you are ready to felt the vest (Figure 9-12).

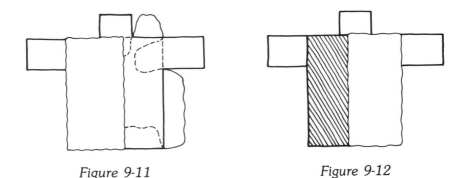

Figure 9-11   Figure 9-12

Step 5. Felting: The wool is now lying in the shape of a vest and is ready to be felted. Starting on the last batt wetted down, felt a small area until you feel the fibers begin to stiffen into felt. Move on to another area until you have worked the whole side of the vest. On vest B, fold the partially felted side over onto itself, fold the plastic sheet over, and work on the other side of the front. After you have worked on the front for 20 to 30 minutes, lay the vest flat, separated by the plastic pattern, and carefully roll it up in a large piece of cloth. Now you can pick up the vest and spin out the water in a washing machine.

After spinning, unroll the vest flat on your work area. Turn it over and repeat the same felting procedure all over the back of the vest. When you have toughened the wool on the back, roll the vest in the cloth again and spin it in the washing machine. Unroll it and continue to felt in areas where needed. Continue this process until the felt is strong enough to be rubbed on the washboard.

Step 6. Fulling: Begin slowly and gently to rub the whole vest on the washboard, one section at a time. Support the areas you are not working on to prevent the felt from stretching out. Continue the fulling procedure until the felt shrinks and toughens. Spin the vest again in the washing machine and try it on.

Check the fit and look to see where more shrinkage is needed. Continue fulling, rinsing, and spinning out the water until the felt is the toughness that you desire and the size is right. The more you rub the felt on the washboard, the smaller and stiffer the material will become. If you want a softer, less stiff material, don't rub it as long on the washboard.

Step 7. Trimming: When you have finished the fulling process, try on the vest and mark where you want to trim the felt. The square pattern requires trimming at the armholes—see the guide to trimming below. After trimming, felt the cut edges with more hot, soapy water. Let the vest dry flat, then decorate it.

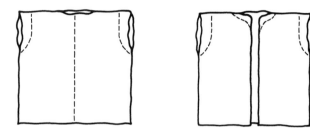

Vest A   Vest B

10
Felt Projects for Children

Making felt is a fun and educational project for children as well as for adults. Children enjoy working with wool right off the sheep. With the wool and hot, soapy water, children can make small shapes of felt by just playing with the wool—with a little imagination, they will find uses for the bits and pieces of felt. This chapter contains simple projects that can be done with children. The projects increase in difficulty—the first ones are appropriate for five- to six-year-olds. When working with children, it is important for them to see results fairly quickly in order to keep their interest. With older children, start with a simple project before trying something more difficult. Once you have gained their interest, they will have the patience to attempt a more time-consuming project.

FELT SAMPLE

A small flat piece of felt can be made in about 10 to 15 minutes. A child could use it for a dollhouse rug, a coaster, or a little washcloth. It can also be sewn onto a shirt for a pocket or decorated with glitter or embroidery.

Making a Felt Sample

Step 1. Card ½ to ¾ ounce of wool according to the instructions in Chapter 2. Make a hot, soapy water solution using 2 cups of hot water and 1 tablespoon of laundry soap.

Step 2. Using all of the wool, make a small batt five to six layers thick. The fibers in each layer should lie crosswise to the fibers in the next layer.

Step 3. Pour ⅛ cup of hot, soapy water into the center of the batt, a little at a time, and wet down the wool in the middle of the batt. Leave 2 inches of dry wool around the edges.

Step 4. Fold the dry wool that extends around the edges over the wet wool, then wet it down over the middle.

Step 5. Now begin to felt the sample. Push down all over the wool with your finger tips—begin gently, and gradually use more pressure as the wool starts to harden. Keep adding hot, soapy water throughout the process. Eventually, you will be pushing down with your whole hand over the entire sample.

Step 6. Now you are ready to do any fulling. Rinse out your sample and check the size and shape. If the wool has turned to material that holds together and does not pull apart easily, you can rub it on the washboard to shrink it more. Add hot, soapy water and then rub it evenly on the washboard.

Step 7. When you have shrunk the sample to the size you want or until it doesn't shrink anymore, rinse it out and set it aside to dry.

Older children can make a felt picture by using dyed or colored wool on the bottom layer of the batt. The dyed wool will felt into the material to give a design. See the instructions in Chapter 12 for incorporating dyed wool into your felt project.

FELT BALL

A felt ball is a more difficult project for a child, but given help with carding, a kindergartener can make one. The ball will bounce when it is dry. A child might decide to use the ball for juggling, as a cat toy, or for many other things.

Making a Felt Ball

Step 1. Card a half ounce of wool. Separate the wool into eight to ten layers.

Step 2. Make a hot, soapy water solution using 2 cups of hot water and one tablespoon laundry soap.

Step 3. Roll one layer of wool into a ball—dip it into the hot, soapy water—and transfer it from one hand to the other, squeezing gently.

Step 4. Add another layer of wool to the ball—wet it—and continue to transfer between your hands, squeezing with more pressure.

Step 5. After adding the third layer, roll the ball between the palms of your hands. Use a lot of pressure so that the layers will begin to felt to each other. The ball will felt properly if you use enough pressure when rolling it between your palms. Continue to add layers of wool to the ball, rolling it between your palms for at least two minutes for each layer. Add hot, soapy water throughout the process.

Step 6. Use dyed wool for the last layer to add color to the ball.

If the wool is not sticking together, use more pressure, and be sure to use plenty of hot, soapy water.

It doesn't matter if a child's ball is a little lumpy—it will still bounce when it is dry. A child can play with the felt ball in the bathtub with soap to shrink it further. When it is wet, the felt ball floats in water.

FELT POCKET

Given a little help with folding the wool, a five-year-old can make a pocket out of felt. Older children can do it themselves. The finished pocket can be made into a little purse or pouch to put things in.

Making a Felt Pocket

Step 1. Card ¾ to 1 ounce of wool, depending on how big you want the pocket to be.

Step 2. Separate the wool into two equal piles, and make two batts of the same size.

Step 3. Make a pattern that is half as wide as the batts and make it as long as the batt.

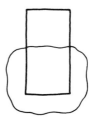

Step 4. Lay one of the batts down on your work surface, then put the pattern on top of it. There should be dry wool extending out on three sides of the pattern.

Step 5. Wet down the wool under the pattern, then fold the dry wool in over the pattern on three sides. Wet down the dry wool over the pattern.

Step 6. Place the second batt on top of the wet wool and pattern, letting the dry wool extend out on the same three sides of the pattern as with the first batt.

Step 7. Wet down the wool only over the pattern, leaving the outside wool dry.

Step 8. Flip the pocket over and fold the dry wool over the wet wool. Mat it down with more hot, soapy water. Now you have the wool in the position for a pocket, and you are ready to felt it.

Step 9. Felt the pocket until the felt is strong enough to be rubbed on the washboard. Then shrink and toughen the felt on the washboard, holding your hand on the inside of the pocket and rubbing it all around.

BERET AND SLIPPERS

Older children can make a felt beret or a pair of slippers. Follow the directions for making a beret or slippers, but instead of using a cloth pattern, use a heavy piece of cardboard for the slipper pattern and wrap it in a plastic bag. For the beret, use a heavy paper plate that you have wrapped in a plastic bag. It is easier for children to felt the project if they can feel the pattern inside.

11
Washing and Durability

How long your felt articles will wear depends on who is wearing them and how thick or tough you made the felt. Children's slippers seem to wear out very quickly in the toes because children like to crawl around on the floor dragging their toes. Adult slippers wear out more quickly under the heel and big toe first because most of the weight is centered in these areas. With normal wear, a pair of adult slippers should last about one to two years. If you wear them as house shoes, they will not last as long.

When you first start wearing your slippers, boots, or mittens, you may find that they shed after wearing them a few times. The coarser wool from a blend of wools does not felt as strongly and will start to come off of the outside and inside surfaces of the article. This should not last long and it eventually stops.

Treat your felt slippers, boots, and mittens as you would any other 100 percent wool garment. They can be dry cleaned or hand washed in cool water using a mild detergent. Squeeze the article gently to avoid shrinking it during washing. When rinsing your felt wearables, don't worry about getting every last drop of soap out—too much wringing may shrink the article further. Squeeze out as much of the water as possible, then blot it dry between towels. Because felt is waterproof, most of the water quickly drains out of it. You can squeeze out the water where it collects, then shape the article and allow it to dry.

Making Soles for Footwear

To extend the life of your slippers or boots, put a sole on them. This also makes them less slippery to walk on. The most popular material to use for a sole is leather or suede. You need a leather needle and buttonhole thread to stitch a sole onto the bottom of each slipper or boot. Allowing the suede to extend up around the edge of the slipper gives more protection for the toe and heel areas. A fairly soft, thin suede accomplishes this best. Ultrasuede (i.e., manmade suede), which can also be used, has an advantage over leather in that it is washable. When hand washing, leather will harden—however, Ultrasuede is just as durable (and as expensive, unfortunately) but may be washed many times and still remains soft. It also requires a leather needle and buttonhole thread for sewing it on. The suede or Ultrasuede sole always outlasts the slippers, so to save on cost, you can reuse these soles for your own and your family's slippers after the felt has worn out.

12
Decorating Felt Wearables

Felt items can be decorated after the felt is formed using many techniques, such as embroidery, appliqué, and dyeing. The decoration can also be worked into the felt during the felting and fulling processes, using colored or dyed fleece or yarn. The following are suggestions for decorating your felt wearables. Depending on your tastes and talents, the possibilities are endless.

Felting Your Design Into the Article

Dyed or Colored Wool (Dry Inlay)

A way to add different colors and textures to your felt wearables is to use dyed or colored wool to contrast with the wool you are using for your batts. Keep the colored wool on top of your second batt for each slipper, boot, mitten, or hat so that the color will end up on the outside of the project. If you want a design to appear all around your piece, as with a hat, place the dyed wool on top of the dry wool after you have placed the second batt on top of the pattern and flipped the hat over. This is in addition to putting the colored wool on top of the second batt. For a marbled effect, use a contrasting color for the last layer of your second batt. As the wool felts, the colored layer will shift and darken as it shrinks to give a marbled look against the solid background.

The type of wool used and the dyeing technique influence the felting quality of dyed wool. Dyed wool used in a felt project may not felt as quickly as the undyed wool. When this is the case, the following suggestions will help you blend the dyed wool into your project:

- Use thin, carded layers instead of clumps of colored or dyed wool.

- Blend some of the dyed wool with undyed wool by carding the two wools together.

- Place a layer of undyed wool over the dyed wool to hold it down. After felting, you can cut into the top layer to reveal the dyed wool underneath. This is another way to make designs on your felt articles.

- Start slowly and gently when felting. Begin by working with the dyed wool under the project. Push down on it from the opposite side of the material. Avoid working directly on the dyed wool.

- Don't give up if it looks like the batting is felting but the dyed wool is just laying on the surface. It will felt more slowly but will eventually be incorporated into the fabric. During the fulling stage, it begins to adhere better.

Colored Yarns

Yarn may be felted onto your project to form designs and add texture. Loosely spun yarns work best. Putting a thin layer of carded wool over the yarn helps to hold it onto the felt. As with the dyed wool, the yarn is arranged on the dry batts before hot, soapy water is added. If the yarn in some spots only partially felts, the yarn can be tacked down later or may be steamed lightly.

Solid Felt Inlay (Wet Inlay)

Shapes of various colors and sizes may be felted into your projects. These felt inlays, which look like appliqué, are incorporated into the felt using the same technique you use when working with dyed or colored wool. A mosaic effect can be obtained using the solid inlay technique. As when using the dyed, carded wool, avoid pushing down directly on the inlay. Instead, work on it from the opposite side of the felt as much as possible.

Instructions for Felt Inlay

Step 1. Make a small batt that is two to three times larger than your inlay design, using hand-carded or drum-carded dyed or colored wool.

Step 2. Pour hot, soapy water in the middle of the batt and wet the wool down to about 1½ inches from the edge. Fold the dry wool around the edges in over the middle and wet it down. Do not continue to push down on the wool (as in the felting technique).

Step 3. With your scissors, carefully cut the wet wool into the shape you want for the inlay.

Step 4. Find the middle layer of the cut-out piece (inlay) and carefully pull the wool apart so you end up with two inlays, each the mirror image of the other.

Step 5. Place the wet inlay (inside side up) on your work surface, then center the dry wool batt on top of it. You may also place the inlay (inside side down) on top of the dry wool into which you plan to felt it.

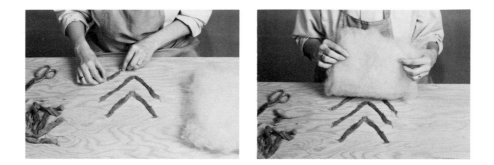

Step 6. Follow the felting technique for your project. Begin gently, then gradually increase the pressure as the inlay begins to stick to the wool. In addition, follow the suggestions for using dyed wool in your felt projects described earlier in this chapter. When fulling, turn the felt article inside out so you are not rubbing the inlay directly against the washboard. This will help make it adhere better to the felt.

Pour hot, soapy water over the middle of the batt.

Wet down the wool in the middle of the batt, leaving two inches dry all around the outside edge.

Fold the dry wool in over the wet wool.

Wet down the wool with hot, soapy water, then push down for five minutes all over the batt.

Lift up the wet wool, with the inlay adhering to it, and turn it over.

Begin to felt the other side, working directly on the inlay, until it felts to the batting. Work gently, then gradually increase the pressure.

Decorating Finished Felt Articles

Embroidery

One of the easiest ways to embellish your felt wearables is to embroider them using colorful yarns. When embroidering on felt, you can take advantage of the thick material by hiding the ends of your yarn within the felt. Make a zigzag stitch within the material, putting the needle back into the same hole that it came out of. In this way, you can avoid having knots on the opposite side of the felt.

The *chain stitch* is commonly used to adorn felt goods. Stitching around the opening of the slipper, boot, or mitten finishes the look. Using the chain stitch, you may decorate your articles by making "fantasy flowers" on the top or sides of your project.

The *blanket stitch* is another popular stitch for decorating felt items. To make this stitch on the edge of an opening, follow the steps below:

1. Hide the end of your yarn within the felt using a zigzag stitch.

2. Push the needle out of the felt about one-half inch below the edge on the outside of the article.

3. Bring the yarn up and around the cut edge and push the needle into the felt on the opposite side, exactly opposite to where it came out on the first side.

4. Push the needle straight up toward the top edge, and push it out through the middle of the yarn.

5. Decide the width you want for the stitch, move the needle over one width, then push the needle straight down into the top edge of the felt and bring it back out on the outside one-half inch from the top edge. Then repeat steps 3 through 5.

Woven Bands

An inkle loom, a backstrap loom, or card weaving can be used to make colorful woven bands for decorating your felt wearables. Various finger-weaving techniques including silentra may be used to make colorful bands, and ribbons can also be used for decoration. Several colors, braided or woven together, make a nice decoration in contrast to the puffy wool felt.

Dyeing Fleece and Finished Felt Articles

The techniques used in dyeing felt are the same as for dyeing other items of wool, including yarn, fleece, and knitted goods. Felt may be dyed using natural dyes or commercial dyes for wool. When using commercial dyes, weak acid dyes that use acetic acid (vinegar) are recommended. Wools dyed with weak acid dyes keep their colors well over time with repeated washings. They are also more resistant to fading. It is important to pick a dye with good washfastness if you are going to use it to dye fleece for felting. The felting process, which requires hot water and soap, may otherwise wash out a dye with less washfastness.

Natural dyes can also be used to dye your finished felt articles or fleece. When dying fleece to be used for felting, be sure to start with medium- or fast-felting wool, or use a blend of wools which will give you good felting quality. If you want your finished article to be a solid color, it is often better to dye it after it is felted, rather than starting with dyed wool. To make a colored design on the felt, you can drop dye onto the finished felt or you can dye fleece in different colors. Allow the dyed fleece to dry, then card it into thin layers and place the layers on top of the second or outside batt for your project (see the earlier description in this chapter of using dyed wool in your project).

Before you dye fleece or your finished felt articles, thoroughly wet the wool first before adding it to the dye bath. Soak it in warm water for at least 20 minutes. After you have prepared the dye bath and added the wool, gradually bring the temperature of the dye bath up to a slow boil. Keep the bath at a slow boil for an hour or more and then allow it to cool gradually. Stir the dye bath regularly during the heating and cooling periods. Wool fibers will continue to absorb some of the dye in the cool-down phase. Slow temperature changes and gentle handling are used when dyeing wool in order to avoid felting. This is important when dyeing fleece, yarn, and knitted goods. When dyeing felt, the process of dyeing can further harden and shrink the felt and at times gives a coarser fabric. With gentle handling in the dye bath, however, the felt should not shrink.

Fleece to be dyed and used for felting can be placed in the dye bath washed or unwashed. Depending on the dye or color used, the unwashed fleece may pick up the dye unevenly. Unwashed fleece may give varied results because of the chemical nature of the materials in it. The combination of the dye bath and the dirty fleece may also cause a reaction that weakens the fibers. The resulting dyed wool is suitable for felting—however, it may not be good for spinning.

When using any dye, whether natural or commercial, it is important to follow the directions which belong with the dye. This ensures that you get the results that you want and that the dye does not become harmful. Even if the dyes are advertized to be nontoxic or safe, follow these guidelines:

- Never dye in pots you will be using for cooking or food.

- Always wear gloves and never touch the dye or dye bath with your bare hands.

- Avoid using your kitchen for dyeing.

Bibliography

Books

Burkett, M. E.; *The Art of the Felt Maker*, Abbot Hall Art Gallery, Kendal, Cumbria, England, 1979.

Carlmann, Alice; *Tovning: filtning og valkning*, Rosenkilde og Bagger, Viborg, Denmark, 1982.

Claessen, Marlie; *Felting: a manual for felting with wool to make clothes or other objects*, Löuet b.v., Lochem, Holland, 1981.

Ekert, Marianne; *Handmade Felt*, Textile Tools, Sunshine Bay, Eastbourne, New Zealand, 1984.

Evers, Inge; *Felt Making: Techniques and Projects*, Lark Books, Ashville, N.C., 1987.

Gordon, Beverly; *Feltmaking*, Watson-Guptill Publications, New York, 1980.

Green, Louise; *Felt Making for the Fiber Artist*, Greentree Ranch Wools, Loveland, Colorado, 1978.

Jørgensen, Annelise Stockflet; *Felting*, 1985.

Wool Science Review 61, International Wool Secretariat, Development Centre, Valley Drive, Ilkley, Yorks, England.

Articles

Fiberarts, November/December 1979.

Fiberarts, July/August 1986.

Ryder, Michael L., "The Evolution of the Fleece", *Scientific American,* January 1987.

Shuttle, Spindle and Dyepot, Winter 1986.

Appendixes

APPENDIX A
Sources of Carded Wool for Felting

The following businesses sell carded wool that can be used for felting. The quality of the wool will vary according to the breed and the blend of wools. Order a small amount to see how quickly it felts before you order a large quantity, as for a vest. The breed of sheep and whether the wool is imported or grown in the United States is included when available. Information is given on whether natural and/or dyed colors are available. Also included is information on how to order. (SASE means a self-addressed stamped envelope.)

Alabama

Little Barn LTD., Inc.
173 McKee Road
Harvest, AL 35749
(800) 542-3275

(Domestic & imported) assorted breeds; batts: white, natural colored and dyed.
To order: Call or write for free catalog.

California

Bar-B-Woolies*
5308 Roeding Rd.
Attn. Dept. F
Hughson, CA 995326
(209)883-0833

Romney/Perendale, Merino, Jacob Navajo-Churro, Calif. Red (imported & domestic); batts for felting.
To order: Call or write. Send $4.00 and SASE for samples.

*Also sells fleece (see Appendix B)

Hobbit Hollow Farm *
P.O. Box 180
Palo Cedro, CA 96073
(916) 549-3749

Breed Crosses include: Targhee, Romney, Lincoln, Finn, Corriedale (domestic); batts for felting - white, natural colored & dyed.
To order: Send SASE or call for information.

Yolo Wool Products
41501 County Road 27
Woodland, CA 95667
(916) 666-1473

(Domestic) White and natural colored; batts and other wool products for felting.
To order: Call or write. Send $2 for sample packet.

Georgia

Norsk Fjord Fiber *
P.O. Box 271
Lexington, GA 30648
(706) 743-5120

Gotland & Spelsau (imported); white & natural colored.
To order: Send $2 for catalog, $5 for fleece and roving samples.

Maine

Halcyon Yarn
12 School Street
Bath, ME
(800) 341-0282

(Domestic & imported) Merino batts; dyed and natural colored wool.
To order: Call or write for information on wool for felting.

Peace Fleece
RR 1, Box 57
Kezar Falls, ME 04047
(800) 482-2841

(Domestic & imported) Blend of wool and mohair batting in natural and over 24 dyed colors.
To order: Call or send $2.00 for "batting" sample card.

Massachusetts

Artist In Me *
17 Madison Avenue
Cambridge, MA 02140
(617) 491-1661

Romney (domestic); white, natural colored and rainbow dyed batts.
To order: Call or write.

R.H. Lindsay Co.
P.O. Box 218
Boston, MA 02124
(617) 288-1155

Romney, Perendale, Merino and other breeds (imported); white and black dyed; sliver carded greasy or washed.
To order: Call or write.

Michigan

Zeilinger Wool Co.
1130 Weiss St.
Frankenmuth, MI 48734
(517)652-2920

(Domestic) White, natural colored and dyed; rainbow batts, carded roving and combed roving top.
To order: Call or write for wool for felting.

New Hampshire

Harrisville Designs
Box 806
Harrisville, NH 03450
(603) 827-3333

(Imported) Dyed, carded wool in a variety of colors.
To order: Call or write.

New Jersey

WoodsEdge Wools *
Box 275
Stockton, NJ08559-0275
(605) 397-2212

(Domestic & imported) White and natural colored. Fine, luster and exotic blend batts. Alpaca in many natural colors.
To order: Call or send for complimentary copy of catalog.

New York

Liberty Ridge Romneys *
Sunny Bixby
R.D. #1, Box 29B
Verona, NY 13478
(315) 337-7217

Romney, Border Leicester (domestic); Custom carded batts, natural and dyed colors; mohair, angora, silk blends, rainbow batts.
To order: Send $3 for color card and sample pack.

Spinners Hill Shop *
Brackett Lake Rd.
P.O. Box 118
Bainbridge, NY 13733
(607) 843-6267

Lincoln cross, Romney cross, Dorset, Rambouillet, Finn (domestic); white and natural colors.
To order: Send SASE and $3 requesting samples of carded wool for felting.

The Woolery *
R.D. #1
Genoa, NY 13071
(800) 441-WOOL
Fax: (315) 497-1542

Carded Merino, Rambouillet and Finn (domestic); white, natural colors and dyed; wool blends.
To order: Call for information. Send $5 for samples of carded wool and blends.

Ohio

Bullen's Wullens
5711 CR#13
Centerburg, OH 43011
(800) 565-7290

(Domestic) Natural white and 50 dyed colors, combed top roving.
To order: Call or write. Send #1 for samples.

Oregon

Woodland Woolworks
262 So. Maple
P.O. Box 400
Yamhill, OR 97148
(800) 547-3725

(Domestic & imported) Roving and batts; Natural and dyed colors.
To order: Call for samples for felting. Catalog available for $3.

Pennsylvania

Wilde Yarns
3737 Main Street
P.O. Box 4226
Philadelphia, PA 19127
(215) 482-8800

(Imported) 5 natural colors, 9 dyed colors.
To order: Send SASE for catalog and $.75 for each sample card (dyed carded or natural carded wool).

South Carolina

The Weaver's Knot *
508 Inlet Drive
Seneca, SC 29672
(800) 680-7747

(Domestic & imported) Natural and white combed tops and sliver.
To order: Call or write. Send $3 for catalog.

Virginia

River Farm *
Rt. 1 Box 471
Fulks Run, VA 22830
(703) 896-5833
(800)USA-WOOL orders

Corriedale & crosses (domestic); Roving and batting in white and a variety of natural colors.
To order: Call or write. Send $1 for catalog; $4.50 for samples.

Wisconsin

Susan's Fiber Shop
N250 Hy A
Columbus, WI 53925
(414) 623-4237

Romney, Corriedale (domestic); White & natural colored; batts and carded roving.
To order: Call or write. Send $2 for samples.

Quilt Batts (needle-punched)

Needle-punched quilt batts may also be used for felting by hand. After felting, the batts form a thin, soft material that is especially nice for baby clothes. The instructions below describe two ways to use the needle-punched batts for felting.

(1) Making a Flat Piece: The needle-punching process makes the batt hold together well enough to be felted in a washing machine. Place the batt (or try a piece first) in a front-loading washing machine with soap and hot water. Be sure to use a front loading machine - the agitator in a top-loading machine will tear the batt apart. Run the machine for three or four minutes, then check the batt. It should be felted. You can make sewn vests, mittens, or other items from the flat piece of felt.

(2) Making Seamless Projects: Start with a pattern one third larger that the finished item. Pull off a piece of batting the size of one of the batts for your project and taper the edges by gently pulling the fibers out. Do the same for the other batts. Follow the directions in the book and shrink the felt on a washboard to make it thicker and stronger.

Source of needle-punched batts:
Taos Mountain Wool Works
P.O. Box 327
Arroyo Hondo, NM 87513
(505) 776-2925

APPENDIX B
Sources of Fleece for Felting

Your best source of fleece is from local farmers in your area. To find them, contact your County Extension Agent for names and addresses of Sheep Growers Associations. These will lead you to individuals who have fleece for sale. Ask for the breeds and cross-breeds described in the book. In addition, describe the characteristics that you are looking for in the wool (see Chapter 1). The businesses in Appendix A whose names are followed by an asterix (*) will also sell fleece that is suitable for felting.

APPENDIX C
Businesses that Card Wool

If you have fleece which you have tested to be good for felting, you may want to send it out to be commercially-carded into batts that can be used for felting. The following businesses will custom-card your wool. Contact them to find out their prices and whether you need to wash the wool before you send it to them.

Alaska

Tails & Yarns of Alaska
P.O. Box 41
Hope, AK 99605
(907) 782-3115

California

Yolo Wool Products
41501 County Road 27
Woodland, CA 95776
(916) 666-1473

Michigan

Frankenmuth Woolen Mill
570 S. Main St.
Frankenmuth, MI 48734
(517) 652-8121

Zeilinger Wool Co.
1130 Weiss St.
Frankenmuth, MI 48734
(517) 652-2920

New Mexico

Taos Valley Wool Mill
P.O. Box 374
Arroyo Hondo, NM 87513
(505) 758-9631

New York

Liberty Ridge Romneys
RD #1, Box 29B
Verona, NY 13478
(315) 337-7217

Fingerlakes Woolen Mill
1193 Stewarts' Corners Rd.
Genoa, NY 13071
(315) 497-1542

The Spinner's Hill Shop
Brakett Lake Rd.
P.O. Box 118
Bainbridge, NY 13733
(607) 843-6267

APPENDIX D is on page 95

(Sources updated 1996)

For updated Appendixes, please send $1 along with a large SASE to Craft Works Publishing, P.O. Box 60703, Palo Alto, CA 94306.

About the Author

Anne Einset Vickrey grew up in the Finger Lakes region of Upstate New York, and presently lives in Northern California. Her Norwegian parents taught her much of their heritage and she was introduced to handcrafts at an early age. Anne learned the Scandinavian felt-making technique in early 1982 when she was shown how to make a pair of felt slippers by a Danish felt-maker. She is otherwise self-taught in the craft; her methods for teaching felt-making to others have been refined by holding numerous workshops throughout the San Francisco Bay Area.

Additional copies of
Felting by Hand
may be ordered from:

Craft Works Publishing
P.O. Box 60703
Palo Alto, CA 94306

Adult-size Mitten

Child-size Mitten

One-half of the Basic

Hat Pattern (place this edge on fold)